# ALASKA'S
# HEROES
## A CALL TO COURAGE

by

NANCY WARREN FERRELL

Alaska Northwest Books®
Anchorage • Portland

Library of Congress Cataloging-in-Publication Data

Ferrell, Nancy Warren.
    Alaska's heroes : a call to courage / by Nancy Warren Ferrell.
        p. cm.
Includes bibliographical references and index.
    ISBN 0-88240-542-X
    1. Alaska Award for Bravery-Heroism.  2.  Decorations of honor—Alaska.
3.  Medals—Alaska.  4.  Heroes—Alaska—Biography.  I. Title.
    CR6253 .F47 2002
    920.0798—dc21

                                                            2002003231

President: Charles M. Hopkins
Associate Publisher: Douglas A. Pfeiffer
Editorial Staff: Timothy W. Frew, Ellen Harkins Wheat, Tricia Brown,
    Jean Andrews, Kathy Matthews, Jean Bond-Slaughter
Copy Editor: Kathleen McCoy
Production Staff: Richard L. Owsiany, Susan Dupere
Cover design: Elizabeth Watson
Interior design: Constance Bollen, cb graphics
Cartographer: Gray Mouse Graphics
Printed in the United States of America

# CONTENTS

★ | ★

## AVIATION RESCUES
13

★ 2 ★

## PUBLIC SAFETY RESCUES
59

★ 3 ★

## WATER AND FIRE RESCUES
73

## ★ 4 ★
## VEHICLE RESCUES
119

## ★ 5 ★
## MORE STORIES OF MEDAL WINNERS
131

## Alaska Statute—Sec. 44.09.090
# STATE OF ALASKA—
# AWARD FOR BRAVERY-HEROISM

(a) The governor is authorized to award a state medal for heroism directly or posthumously to any citizen of the state in recognition of a valorous and heroic deed performed in the saving of a life or for injury or death or threat of injury or death incurred in the service of the state or the citizen's community or on behalf of the health, welfare, or safety of other persons. The medal shall be awarded by the governor with an appropriate ceremony.

(b) The governor shall make arrangements for the designing of the medal for heroism through a statewide design competition participated in by the school children of the state. (1 ch 12 SLA 1965)

# DEDICATION

*Alaska's Heroes: A Call to Courage* is dedicated to all those people who put their lives on the line for someone else.

Photo credits:  pp. 1 and 101: U.S. Coast Guard; p. 8: Robert Brantley, courtesy of David Lancaster; p. 12: Courtesy of Fellowship Ministries; pp. 16, 19: Dick Odgers; p. 21: Al Hershberger; p. 23: Courtesy of Kearlee Ray Wright; p. 25: Courtesy of George Jackinsky; p. 29: Courtesy of the Alaska Department of Public Safety; p. 32: Courtesy of Joyce Sarles; p. 36: Nancy Warren Ferrell; p. 39: Courtesy of Wanda Gard; p. 43: Courtesy of Fellowship Ministries; p. 47: Courtesy of Nancy McGuire, the *Nome Nugget*; p. 49: Courtesy of Fellowship Ministries; p. 54: Fish and Wildlife Protection Service, courtesy of Patricia Stimson-Wilson; p. 56: Courtesy of Bob Larson; p. 58: Courtesy of Cliff and Nancy Hollenbeck; p. 62: Courtesy of Don Peterson; p. 65: Courtesy of Cliff and Nancy Hollenbeck; p. 69: Courtesy of the Alaska State Troopers, Kevin Waugh, photographer; p. 72: Courtesy of Alaska National Guard; p. 75: Andrew Haviland, courtesy of H. Vernon Slwooko Jr.; p. 76: Courtesy of Andrew Haviland; p. 80: Andrew Haviland, courtesy of H. Vernon Slwooko Jr.; p. 85: Reflections Alaska; p. 86: Courtesy of Vera Howarth; p. 90: © Matt Hage, *Fairbanks Daily News-Miner*; p. 93: Courtesy of Al Rothfuss; p. 94: Alaska Division of Tourism; p. 105: Courtesy of Fairweather Fish, Inc.; p. 108: Nancy Warren Ferrell;  p. 112: Courtesy of Betty Olanna; p. 117: *Fairbanks Daily News-Miner*; p. 118: Robert Brantley photo, courtesy of David Lancaster; p. 122: Robert Brantley photo, courtesy of David Lancaster; p. 125: Courtesy of Tom Burgess; p. 128: David Graham; p. 130: Alaska Governor's Office.

# ACKNOWLEDGMENTS

A number of organizations found photographs and information, or directed me to those who could help. Mentioning a few, the author thanks the Alaska National Guard, the Alaska State Troopers, the Alaska Division of Fire Prevention, the United States Coast Guard, the Alaska Department of Military and Veterans Affairs, Fellowship Publishing (Tempe, Arizona), the Federal Aviation Administration, the Ketchikan City Museum, the Nome Police Department, the Ketchikan Police Department, and the Alaska Archives and Records Center.

Without fail, the Alaska State Library came through, the staff always willing to assist. Thanks to my writing group (Susi Gregg Fowler, Jean Rogers, Bridget Smith), who helped with direction on this book over the years; to Linda Perez of the governor's office, who was there at busy times with ready answers; and to my sounding board, my husband, Ed Ferrell.

The author is especially grateful to so many people—those who recalled sad or happy memories, those who helped with information and photographs. It is the people contact, not the paper research, that personalizes these emergencies. Thank you.

Anderson, Dave—Arizona
Andrews, Mechelle—Gambell
Bania, John—Soldotna
Benedek, Vera—Kiana
Blades, Clint—Sitka
Blades, Jill—Sitka
Blades, Jim—Sitka
Bloes, Roy—Anchorage
Brantley, Robert—Georgia
Burdick, Terri—Soldotna
Burgess, Tom—Fairbanks
Canterbury, Chuck—Fort Richardson
Champion, Errol—Juneau
Chisum, Petie—Arizona
Christensen, Craig N.—FortRichardson
Colgan, Lee—Anchorage
Collinsworth, Sherry—Nikiski
Comer, (Clifford) Keith—Massachusetts

Cornfield, Robin—Anchorage
Coulter, George—Oregon
Cusack, Bob—Iliamna
Cushing, Michael—Juneau
Dietsche, Cary—Wisconsin
Douglass, Linda—Fairbanks
Edgren, Rose—Delta Junction
Eldridge, Pam—Anchorage
Gard, Wanda—Michigan
Geary, Evans—Kotzebue
Gentile, Jerry—Juneau
Graham, David—Kenai
Greaves, Walter—Anchorage
Guthrie, Emily—New Mexico
Haile, Donald—Buckland
Haller, Mike—Fort Richardson
Harper, Roy—Wyoming
Harvey, Eric—Eagle River

Haviland, Andrew—White Mountain
Heath, Marge—Fairbanks
Hollenbeck, Nancy Davis—Washington
Holst, John—Sitka
Howarth, Vera—Soldotna
Jackinsky, George—Kasilof
Jacobsen, Robert—Juneau
James, Harry—Juneau
Kauer, Bob—Nome
Kiyutelluk, Alfred—Shishmaref
Koechlein, Kevin—Talkeetna
Kramer, Kevin—Juneau
Lafferty, Dick—Florida
Lake, Gretchen—Fairbanks
Lancaster, David—Alabama
LaPorte, Tim—Iliamna
Larson, Robert—Anchorage
Lee, Fred—Buckland
Lee, Raymond—Buckland
Leipzig, Charles—Wisconsin
Lind, Peter—Juneau
Lyons, Tod—Kodiak
Massey, Walt—Juneau
Moon, M. Scott—Soldotna
Murphy, Sigurd E.—Fort Richardson
Newland, Lisa—Washington
O'Brien, Patrick—Juneau
Odgers, Dick—Soldotna
Olanna, Betty Jean—Nome
Olanna, Penny—Nome
Oles, Randy—Nome
Olsen, Mike—Juneau
Pence, Gretchen—Juneau
Pentilla, Eric—Nome
Perez, Linda—Juneau
Peterson, Diane—Seattle
Peterson, Don—Seattle
Prinzing, Mary Jean—Minnesota
Prinzing, Randy—Minnesota

Prinzing, Rick—Minnesota
Richardson, Claire—Juneau
Riley, Sandy—Ketchikan
Romano, Marilyn—Fairbanks
Rothfuss, Albert—Copper Center
Rowe, Chris—Nome
Rowe, Jim—Nome
Russell, Alex—Soldotna
Rutman, Jason—Kotzebue
Rutman, Robert—Fairbanks
Sarles, Joyce—Juneau
Saylor, Carl—Virginia
Schron, Dave—California
Shaindlin, Jean—Anchorage
Shaub, Rusty—Juneau
Slwooko, H. Vernon—Gambell
Storm, Joette—Anchorage
Swanson, Chicky—Kotzebue
Swearingen, Dave—Sitka
Swedberg, Pam—Soldotna
Tunks, Jeff—Louisiana
Van Cleave, Richard—Ketchikan
Van Doren, Kirk—Homer
Van Horn, Kathy—Sitka
Vick, Marit—Fairbanks
Vogel, Daniel—North Dakota
Westlock, Bill—Emmonak
Wien, Merrill—Washington
Wien, Richard—Fairbanks
Williams, Lew Jr.—Ketchikan
Williams, Tina—Ketchikan
Wilson, Trish Stimson—Cordova
Wiltrout, Gary—Idaho
Winston, Walter—Fairbanks
Worley, Mark—Washington
Wright, Kearlee Ray—Soldotna
Yerex, Bob—Sitka
Zartarian, Mark—New Hampshire

When accidents occur on remote stretches of Alaska's highways, other travelers often render aid until professional rescuers can get to the scene.

★

# ANSWERING THE CALL

*"In life a moment happens
and no day after that is ever the same again."*

—Kieran O'Farrell, Wings of Alaska

## What makes a hero?

Ask that question of a young boy, and he's likely to tell you about a costumed character with amazing superpowers. To the teenager on a diet of action movies, the hero is the muscle-bound gunman in search of his own brand of justice. And if you ask an older man, he'll retell the story of a friend who died in defense of his country long ago.

We also recognize the faces of everyday heroes around us: the firefighters and police who day after day respond to emergencies as small as a fender-bender and as overwhelming as the events of September 11, 2001. And the Coast Guard and other military services who are on call and risk their lives for the safety and freedom of others.

And then there are the ordinary people who rise one morning expecting another typical day, and instead find themselves performing CPR on a stranger, carrying children out of a burning building, or digging through rubble in search of survivors.

This book is filled with stories of those kinds of people—the professionally trained rescuers as well as the individuals who instantly respond with their hearts. People who have been spurred to action in a place where the distance, climate, travel, and basic living conditions create a set of circumstances even more dangerous. In 1965, the state's legislature authorized the governor to recognize "a valorous and heroic deed" on behalf of the state or its citizens. Since then, governors have gathered citizens to honor these deeds and present the State of Alaska Award for Bravery-Heroism.

Each story in this book recounts the drama and circumstances that thrust an individual, or sometimes a team of people, into the moment of urgency, the moment of great personal risk for the benefit of another.

The stories vary widely. In one case, an entire Alaska Native village was honored for the way it responded to a plane crash. A number of the medals were awarded posthumously. Perhaps the saddest and bravest was a ten-year-old boy who returned to a burning house to save his aunt, and died there.

Men, women, and young people are honored. Who could be braver than Alaska State Trooper Rose Edgren, who faced down a violent father to protect his terrified children? Or the twenty-two-year-old flight attendant who remained with her aircraft after it was hijacked by a convicted felon?

Some stories are especially Alaskan, such as the seven Yupik hunters stranded on icebergs in the north Bering Sea for almost a month. Or the fate of the *Dora H.*, loaded with thirty thousand pounds of halibut before she sank south of Kodiak Island.

Amazing teamwork marks many rescues. A wonderful example comes from the village of Buckland, just below the Arctic Circle, where four teenage boys struggled together to save and revive a younger lad who had fallen through the ice. Or the four rescuers who literally plucked seven missionaries from the Bering Sea after their plane ran out of gas—and ferried several to shore as they clung to the rescue helicopter's skids.

Humility seems to be an almost universal trademark of those honored. When one man pulled a woman from her burning car, a trooper responding to the scene recommended him for the award. The man was humble about his efforts. "I was young," he said. "I reacted instinctively, just doing what had to be done." And, in sentiments that echo our renewed appreciation for firefighters and rescue workers, he added, "I just put my life on the line one time. Others do it all the time."

What would you have done? As you read these accounts, you'll notice that, like you, none of these people was gifted with amazing superpowers. They just answered the call.

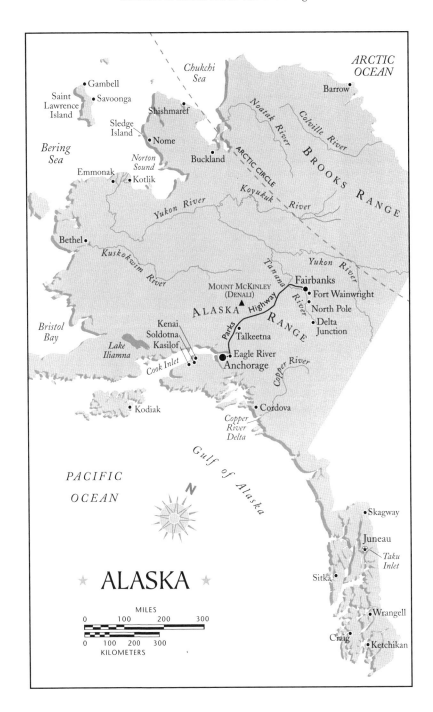

The rescue helicopter piloted by Eric Pentilla of Evergreen Helicopters
came to the rescue of crash victims afloat in the Bering Sea.

# AVIATION RESCUES

For a state as spectacular and far-flung as Alaska, airplanes and helicopters—the essential tools of aviation—are its lifeblood. Collected here are six dramatic stories detailing daring rescues of downed passengers and aircraft. From the account of seven missionaries successfully scooped from the frigid Bering Sea, to the heartbreaking loss of a toddler as a floatplane flipped on takeoff at Lake Iliamna, to the untimely death of a courageous rescuer whose search helicopter crashed near Cordova—readers will be impressed by the intuitive and unselfish efforts of these recipients of the State of Alaska Award for Bravery-Heroism.

# AGAINST ALL ODDS

Lake Iliamna, 1990

Lake Iliamna, west of the Aleutian Mountain Range, not only is the second-largest freshwater lake within U.S. borders (Lake Michigan is first), but it supports the largest runs of red salmon in the world. This pristine wilderness is a playground for fishermen, big-game hunters, and photographers.

Pilot and master guide Robert Cusack owns Cusack's Alaska Lodge, a wilderness resort, on the shore of Intricate Bay there. Originally from Illinois, Cusack spent thirty years in an Alaska hunting/fishing operation. In winter Cusack resides with his family on Mercer Island in Washington, but in summer he opens the Alaska lodge and flies clients to popular fishing and hunting spots close by.

Early one July Sunday, an afternoon wind picked up over Lake Iliamna, churning the waters. Cusack had flown a party of clients to a hot fishing spot for rainbows that day, and later brought the fishermen back. He was scheduled to return a group of clients to Anchorage the same evening, but those gusting winds convinced Cusack not to fly. He knew such winds could create "cat's paws," with wind-shear currents twisting away from regular winds, causing particularly dangerous weather. He thought it best to wait for better conditions.

Because of this decision, Cusack was surprised to hear a small plane engine rev up around a point of land near the lodge. Those tricky winds gusting up to thirty miles per hour on the lake could be more than trouble. "I can't believe anybody'd take off in this stuff," he thought to himself.

Curious and concerned, he stepped outside to watch. A strong wind blew against his face, and he noticed two- to three-foot waves on the boiling water. Weather like that could make for a difficult takeoff.

Cusack's fellow pilot and friend Dr. Alex Russell from Soldotna was chopping wood for the lodge's sauna and heard the aircraft. He, too, was amazed that anyone would take a plane up in such a hazardous situation.

In a secluded cove near the lodge, pilot Ron Kaylor checked the instrument panel on his Cessna 185 floatplane. Son-in-law Dave Elliott sat beside him in the cockpit. Seated behind were his wife, Jean Kaylor, and next to her their daughter, Michelle Elliott. On the women's laps perched the Kaylors' grand-children, Aubrey, three, and Kenan, six. The weekend had been great at the cabin, but now the family was headed back to Anchorage. Kaylor revved the engine and pushed forward.

At the lodge, Bob and Alex watched in disbelief as a blue and white private floatplane emerged from a point of land and lifted off the lake, clearing to about fifty feet. Suddenly the motor sputtered and stalled, the right wing dropping. The pilot pulled the aircraft level, but then the right wing dipped again, diving sharply down at about sixty miles per hour. As the right float slammed the surface, followed by the right wing, the Cessna wheeled over with an arching spray fanning through the air. The whole incident happened so quickly, only about four hundred yards from Cusack's lodge.

Both Alex and Bob, along with Mike Larson of Washington and Dan Vogel, a client from North Dakota, ran for the dock, launched an eighteen-foot skiff, and took off at full throttle. Cutting through the chop, the boat's bow pointed toward the back end of the Cessna's tail, the only plane part showing above the water.

Several minutes passed as they sped to the accident. The gusty winds roiled the waters, making them murky; Bob could tell it would be difficult finding anything under the surface.

As the skiff glided up, the men saw an older man swimming and diving at the site. Pilot Ron Kaylor appeared dazed, in shock. Bob asked how many were in the plane and was told five. Just as he spoke, Michelle Elliott's head burst through the surface, her mouth gasping, screaming, calling hysterically for her babies. Dropping under again, she surfaced once more, crying, this time signaling she held something under the water.

Bob Cusack stepped onto the Cessna's pontoon and dove into the forty-five-degree water. The icy shock popped him straight up again like a cork. Holding his breath, under he went another time. He had figured right: he couldn't see anything. The cove boiled with energy, picking up mud from the bottom that obscured the waters. The plane had flipped, turning everything upside down and causing more confusion. The search had to be done by feel alone.

Just under the surface, Cusack gripped the woman's arm, following it down underwater, groping to a small foot, sliding down the thin leg of a youngster. Something had caught the head or shoulders of the child. The pilot dove with Bob, and between them, feeling their way along as best they could, the two worked the body free and shot up. The boy—Kenan—had been under at least six or seven minutes by then.

Besides owning a lodge, Bob Cusack is a well-known pilot in Southcentral Alaska.

Shivering at the surface, icy cold himself, Bob shifted around and handed the body up to the doctor in the skiff. The youngster's face was as blue as the sky, and he showed no vital signs—no pulse, no breathing. Russell placed him across a seat to begin CPR. Rough water conditions in an open skiff made the procedure very difficult, but Mike and Dan helped maneuver the boat, keeping it next to the wreck and holding it as steady as possible. By then swimmers had helped Michelle Elliott into the boat, too. No sooner was she in than she jumped out again, determined to save her other child. Dan grabbed her hair as she landed in the water, struggled with her, and hauled her back into the skiff.

With Alex Russell working on him, Kenan came around in a few minutes, gasping for air and screaming. The doctor passed him to his anxious mother. Cusack dove again. The worrying thought flashed through his mind that someone might, in their desperation, grab him and pull him down, too. Panic worked that way. Several times he and the pilot surfaced, gulped in air, and dove again.

"The passengers," Cusack wondered, "where are the other passengers, including the little girl?"

On the surface, another skiff neared, but Russell waved it away; grinding boat motors and people popping to the surface were not a safe combination.

Underwater, Cusack searched by feel. He fumbled upon another body, an adult, he could tell. It took five dives to free Jean Kaylor, work her out the plane door, and bring her to the surface. From her dead weight, he knew she was gone.

Someone in the boat grabbed the body and dragged her on board the skiff. Her very blue color gave little hope.

"Not breathing," the doctor remarked. "No pulse." But he laid the grandmother out as best he could against the side of the boat, tried to keep her airway clear, and began lifesaving measures. The small skiff was quickly becoming overcrowded. Russell found it difficult to see if his emergency procedures made any headway.

Back in the water, down Cusack went again, in spite of his own numbness. He had a young daughter himself, and all he could think about was locating the missing girl.

Feeling, tracing objects underwater, the pilot and Bob fumbled upon another adult and tried to release him. Again and again they dove, but the plane gripped Dave Elliott and he could not be freed. The victim must have been alive for a while, for they later discovered he had kicked out the inner windshield's Plexiglas, and his leg was wedged in the V-brace strut outside. The little girl, Aubrey, could not be found.

The next time Cusack surfaced, Alex could tell that Bob showed signs of hypothermia himself—his speech was slurred, his actions clumsy. He told Bob the older woman would surely die of hypothermia if they did not speed her to the lodge and warm her up. They had done all they could, and Alex insisted they give up the search or there might be more victims.

Crowded in the skiff, they crossed the bay toward the lodge. The doctor continued CPR and noticed signs that his efforts with Jean Kaylor were producing results. By the time they reached land, she had vomited and was breathing. After they stretched her out on the dock, Russell held her head, and her pulse stabilized. She needed warmth next.

In the lodge, Michelle Elliott and Kenan recovered quickly once warmed up. Michelle's mother, Jean Kaylor, remained disoriented and extremely hypothermic for quite a while, but progressively improved.

A lawyer, Dan Vogel thought it best to document events that evening. He sat down and detailed the particulars—who was involved, what had happened, when, and what was done.

That evening after the rescue, several men motored out to the downed Cessna and tried to float it closer to shore for more accessibility. It drifted only a short distance, however. As they worked, the bottom part of a seat floated by; searchers found no other debris. Authorities arranged for a dive team from Soldotna to recover the bodies the next day.

Owner and operator of the downed craft Ron Kaylor, a pilot for twenty years, said he had owned the Cessna for one week. The aircraft had previously been sunk and then rebuilt, he stated in the police report. He felt something wrong on liftoff and had had the problem since purchasing the plane. A later National Transportation and Safety Board report cited the pilot for several possible causes of the accident, dealing with aircraft overloading, not following procedures, not enough seats with belts, and poor pilot judgment.

"Pilot's unfamiliarity with local wind patterns may have contributed to the plane crash," Federal Aviation Administration spokesman Paul Steucke said in the *Anchorage Daily News.*

As was normal for Lake Iliamna, the wind evened off late that Sunday evening, and a De Havilland Beaver from Iliamna Air Taxi, piloted by Tim LaPorte, flew safely across the 20 miles of lake to Cusack's lodge. The turnaround flight transported survivors to Iliamna, where a turboprop air ambulance medevacced them 170 miles to Providence Hospital in Anchorage.

On Monday divers from the Nikiski Fire Department scoured underwater for the remaining victims. They brought up the body of David Elliott and dove under the plane for the little girl, but they could not locate her in the expected area.

Widening the search, divers discovered little Aubrey Elliott near the center of the small bay. Authorities assumed she had been thrown from the plane and sank to the bottom. The plane in turn had drifted westward toward shore and away from the child.

Bob Cusack told his wife, Lula, to keep their daughter inside the lodge when they brought up the body of little Aubrey. So Lula watched alone and later sadly remarked how the dead girl's hair resembled their own daughter's. Cusack was relieved that the child had not been in the plane, for he would have felt guilty about missing her if she had died there.

In hindsight, participants speculated that if the little girl had been wearing a flotation vest, she might have popped to the surface when thrown from the Cessna or, if she had been belted in the plane, Cusack would have found her.

The rescuers sensed a satisfying elation at helping the survivors, while experiencing a deep regret at not being able to save the others. All the freed victims of the crash survived.

Corporal James Farrell of the Alaska State Troopers recommended Cusack for the hero's medal; the governor's office concurred. For his unselfish acts with risk to his own life, Robert Cusack received the State of Alaska Award for Bravery-Heroism from Governor Walter Hickel in Anchorage one year later. The accompanying citation read: "To Robert A. Cusack for his heroic efforts to save the passengers of a small plane which had crashed upside down in Lake Iliamna on July 1, 1990."

Once righted and pulled to shore, damage to the Cessna 185 is clearly visible.

The other rescuers—Alex Russell, Mike Larson, and Dan Vogel—also received commendations. In addition, a congratulatory letter from President George Bush and his wife, Barbara, arrived for each.

Dr. Alex Russell presently teaches flying and uses the Iliamna rescue as an example in his classes.

"A rescuer must be prepared to be innovative in the wilderness," the doctor emphasizes. Safety methods and tactics that seem pointless on the surface, he tells his students, have a practical base in the wilderness and should be followed. And, he adds, "The weather is greater than all of us and it will not change just because you want it to. Wait for favorable conditions before leaving a safe haven."

How did the ordeal affect Robert Cusack? The rescue proved a heavy emotional experience all around. Besides feeling badly about not saving the little girl after the crash, Cusack realized how vulnerable humans are. Mostly he has become especially cautious, taking the job of flying even more seriously. Cusack continues guiding from his resort.

Rescuer Dan Vogel said later that the right people were at the right spot at the right time. Another place and time and those who'd lived might have died. Russell, he said, with Larson's help, brought two people back from the dead. And Vogel had nothing but praise for Cusack. "He did an amazing job. Without thinking, he dove right in. It was an amazing effort." ★

# RETURN FROM DEATH

## Kasilof, 1977

Pilot John "Chad" Nepple prepared his twin-engine Beech Bonanza for a flight to the fishing village of Tyonek on a summer day in 1977. No problem flying the fifty miles across Cook Inlet and back with a load of salmon for the Kasilof cannery. He had done it before. Besides, weather on the northwest side of the Kenai Peninsula proved no problem either—not a cloud marred the warm, calm August day.

Knowing eighteen-year-old Kearlee Ray Wright was learning to fly, Nepple asked him to go along. "Sure," said Wright, happy for the experience.

At Tyonek, men loaded waxed one-hundred-pound boxes of fish through the rear of the plane. Though the workers stacked the cartons neatly, they were not tied down. Wright, more than ever aware of flight rules just then, knew this was against regulations, but he kept quiet.

On the return to Kasilof, Nepple allowed Wright to take the flight over Cook Inlet to gain more flying experience. Nervous about the loose fish boxes in the rear, Wright finally asked Nepple about it. The pilot grew angry and took the wheel. After that, Wright remained silent.

About 10:00 P.M. that dusky Friday evening, the Bonanza made its approach over the quiet Kasilof airstrip. Losing elevation on the first run, the plane flew too far down the runway for a safe touchdown. Nepple pulled back on the stick to gain altitude for another try, but because of overloading the aircraft did not readily respond. In that moment, the fish boxes in the rear shifted, and Nepple lost control. The Bonanza hit the gravel airstrip, scraped along the runway, sparks flying, and plowed into the trees. A fire broke out on impact.

A half mile away, commercial fisherman George Jackinsky kicked off boots in his kitchen, tired after a long day on the water. He had asked his son, John, and daughter, Lisa, to drive his fishing helper home. Jackinsky expected them back any time.

Jackinsky, then well into his middle years, had long been a self-confident man. After losing his Polish father and Aleut mother as a teenager, George served a stint in the Air Force, working in Europe and Africa before settling in

Overall damage to the crashed Beech-18.

Kenai as a commercial fisherman. He was resourceful, ever positive. A close friend said of the man, "[He] doesn't know defeat . . . he won't tolerate defeat." Those qualities were soon tested.

That August evening, Jackinsky had no sooner set his boots down when John burst through the kitchen door, alerting him that a plane had just crashed and a fire had started. He'd dropped Lisa near the blaze to see if she could help. Throwing on clothes, George sped with John to the airstrip.

When they arrived, flames licked at branches, shot to the treetops, and lit the whole area, heat from the inferno warming the chill evening air. Besides smoke, the entire clearing smelled of fuel. "I thought it was hopeless," George Jackinsky said, recalling the blazing wreck. "I knew, I just knew, that the plane was going to explode." Nevertheless, he jumped from the truck and pulled his daughter back.

Lisa yelled, "There're people in there, Dad." Jackinsky could make out a head bobbing in the cockpit.

Without considering the danger, Jackinsky reacted. Realizing there was no way of reaching the victims through the front, he spun around, diving for the rear cargo door. Jerking on the handle as hard as he could, he found the door would not budge. Someway, Jackinsky mustered superstrength and, amazingly, tore the door off its hinges—a three-hundred-pound door! Sliding into the plane, Jackinsky inched forward on his belly, fighting to reach the copilot in front. Mounds of jumbled boxes and slippery fish blocked his way, and the sound of the fire whooshed through the plane like a blowtorch. He climbed and scrabbled forward, the heat nearly unbearable. Finally he reached forward to touch a shoulder.

For Kearlee Ray Wright, time had stopped.

After the crash, Wright's body sat in the burning cockpit. None of the noise, the smell, the feel of fire and broken bones touched him. Instead, his conscious, thinking being left the plane. He remembered floating over the trees, feeling exhilarated and watching everything below.

"To the right was a gauzy white curtain or veil of some kind. I knew there were people—I could hear them on the other side as I floated above. I could hear my dead grandfather's voice."

Looking below, Wright saw his body in the plane. He watched his clothing afire, sensed the deadly danger. Still, above, he experienced none of that. He felt out of time.

All this must have happened in uncounted measure, for Jackinsky had not paused in his rescue efforts. The instant Jackinsky reached forward in the burning cockpit and touched Wright's shoulder, time returned.

Wright said his floating body above drifted down into his physical body below, feeding into his legs, his body, his arms, his head. Once his whole conscious self returned to the plane, he nearly collapsed from the searing heat, the choking smoke, his burning eyes. Pain overwhelmed him. Through the uproar in the cockpit, he thought he heard Nepple next to him say, "Don't leave me here."

Jackinsky grabbed at Wright's wrist but it slid out of his hand—too bloody. He grabbed again, this time gripping, tugging, and hefting him back. Jackinsky yanked and pulled until Wright came out of the seat. He was half conscious, so he struggled, trying to help Jackinsky. Some clue right then flashed in Jackinsky's mind that the copilot's spine might be broken.

Finally Jackinsky hauled Wright back through the fish, over the boxes, and, with Lisa's help, dragged him to the wingtip outside. People said Wright screamed then, "Save Chad—he's still alive—save Chad!"

Wright struggled on the ground, and Lisa held him down, almost sitting on him, trying to keep him still. "Get Chad!" he kept yelling. Other people had gathered around, trying to help some way.

Free of the wreck, Jackinsky stared back toward the burning mass. Where he had reacted instinctively the first time, he now had his senses. He realized

Kearlee Ray Wright sits in the cockpit of a Boeing 727 rented as a trainer in Los Angeles about 1986. Wright piloted planes for twenty years after the accident.

the engine might—probably would—blow up any second. He knew how impossible it was getting the copilot out. Besides, the pilot was probably dead already; he almost had to be. How could he live through that?

"I can't do it, Lisa," Jackinsky said. "I can't go back in there."

But he could not be sure the pilot was dead, and he thought he heard the man cry out. He had to try. Back into the burning plane he lunged.

The stink of cooking fish hit him; the heat alone nearly drove him back. Trying not to think, Jackinsky slid through the fish, over the boxes, and grabbed for the pilot. Freeing him seemed impossible. Yet calling on that superstrength, Jackinsky hefted Nepple up and over the seat. Scrambling backward, sure something would blow now, Jackinsky whipped the pilot through the fish and out the cargo entrance.

No sooner had they both cleared the plane when a tremendous blast shot straight up into the trees. The whole front of the plane exploded, and "the cabin blew like a bomb." An oxygen bottle under the pilot's seat had ignited, but it shot up, not out. If it had exploded out, the fire would have engulfed anyone near the plane. As it turned out, the pilot's pants caught fire, and Jackinksy remembered stomping on them to put the flames out. It was nothing but a miracle Jackinsky was not injured.

By then an ambulance and paramedics had arrived. Rescuers loaded the victims and rushed them to the Soldotna Hospital.

Wright later learned the crash had broken his back in four places, exposed his spinal cord, left his scalp hanging by a thread, and caused other serious injuries. After a few days at the Soldotna Hospital, where a medical team stabilized him, physicians medevacced him along with his mother and nurses to Anchorage's Providence Hospital. There doctors completed six hours of surgery on his back.

As he lay in bed recuperating, Wright received several photographs of the mangled airplane from an anonymous party. On the back of one was the note: "You got your life back—now make it count." After a month, the hospital released Wright in a body cast.

Wright survived his ordeal, graduating from surgery to body cast to complete use of his body. He still suffers a few aches and leftover pains at times, but has learned to live with them. Because of his injuries, his family thought he would never fly again. However, as soon as he could, even before he'd completely healed, he maneuvered back into the cockpit and practiced flying until he earned his pilot's license. Airport workers would pick him up, cast and all, place him in the plane, belt him in, and there he taught student fliers. By the time he reached age thirty, Wright had logged fourteen thousand miles with a perfect safety record. The out-of-body episode, however, changed his outlook on life and death; he does not fear death or even pain the way he did before.

Wright was one of the first people to have a Harrington metal rod installed in his broken back. The problem comes now when he flies on commercial flights. Every time he steps through the security frame at the airport, all the alarms go off. Wright has to practically disrobe to prove there are no weapons concealed on his body.

Pilot John "Chad" Nepple survived the crash but was confined to a wheelchair. As of a few years ago, he worked as a flight controller in Florida.

For Jackinsky's heroic act of saving the lives of Wright and Nepple, Governor Jay Hammond granted him the State of Alaska Award for Bravery-Heroism. The Alaska Legislature added its commendation: ". . . for his brave and courageous efforts. . . ." Lisa and John also received official citations.

For months after the crash, the ordeal haunted both George and Lisa Jackinsky. In the middle of the night, fiery dreams invaded George's sleep, waking him. Thinking something to drink would calm his nerves, he would pad to the kitchen and brew coffee. Shortly after, Lisa would come wandering in, upset by her own fiery nightmares.

At the medal award presentations, from left: John Jackinsky, Governor Jay Hammond, Lisa Jackinsky, and George Jackinsky.

George and his wife, who have celebrated their fiftieth wedding anniversary, continue to live in Kasilof, although George recently retired from commercial fishing. The 1977 rescue affected him in that he takes life more seriously now, realizing how fragile humans are.

A year or so after the experience, Jackinsky said, he was strolling down the street in Soldotna when suddenly a woman hurried up and wrapped her arms around him. She proved to be Wright's wife, Jeannie, thanking him for saving her husband's life. ★

# BEYOND THE CALL

## Saint Lawrence Island, 1975

Alaska State Trooper Gilbert Pelowook of Savoonga fastened his seat belt as Wien Flight 99 gained altitude. A scheduled passenger had given up his seat to make room for the officer, summoned to Gambell on a case that day in August 1975. Thirty-eight-year-old Pelowook glanced out the window at the gray, drizzly afternoon that shrouded Saint Lawrence Island. He, along with twenty-eight other passengers, settled down for the last hop of the once-a-week, one-hour trip from Nome.

Saint Lawrence Island, a volcanic mountaintop, is closer to Russia than to mainland Alaska, rising from the Bering Sea about 130 miles southwest of Nome, Alaska. Shadowed by a rocky hill to the east, the town of Gambell itself rests at the northwest tip of the island.

Residents of Saint Lawrence live primarily by subsistence, retaining their Siberian Yup'ik customs and language. Since ancient times they have understood the value of sharing, of responsibility for those around them during good times and bad.

Growing up on the island, Pelowook personally knew about caring for others. Even as a teenager, with his father dead of German measles and his mother from childbirth, Gilbert, as the oldest sibling in the family, supported and cared for his five younger brothers and a sister. He matured into a quiet, modest, competent man, joining the National Guard and later training as a state trooper.

Experience had tested Pelowook's bravery only three months earlier when he responded to the May crash of a private plane in which six people died on a takeoff accident outside Savoonga. Pelowook, one of the rescuers, helped free the pilot from the aircraft, but the man died soon afterward. "He [Pelowook] did all he could to save the passengers but to no avail, for they appeared to have died on impact. Only pilot Chuck Fagerstrom lived and then for just a few minutes," the *Nome Nugget* reported.

On this Saturday in August, rain fell through light fog as the twin turboprop jet approached Gambell in the afternoon. The trooper gazed out the cabin window ahead, observing the new housing being constructed in the village. Coming up directly in front of the aircraft was the six-hundred-foot hill.

Pelowook had taken this trip many times before, so he grew alert as he stared out the window. Something was wrong . . . the elevation; the plane flew lower than normal. "I know our direction is toward the mountain," Pelowook told the *Anchorage Daily News*. He just had time to grab his seat belt, yank it tight, and brace, before the plane slammed into "the upper part of a six-hundred-foot mesa-like promontory some one and one-half miles east of the Gambell airstrip."

Villagers below heard the collision and immediately knew what had happened. Their instant reaction was to help—the strangers on board, as well as sons and daughters, friends and relatives. Residents snatched up blankets, bedding, clothing, first-aid supplies. Grabbing anything usable for makeshift stretchers, the people hurried on their way in minutes by foot or on three-wheeled vehicles.

For a short time after the crash, Pelowook lost consciousness. Slowly recovering, the trooper found himself flat on his face, still strapped in his seat, partially covered with debris. It took a moment adjusting to the dusky light and the strange world surrounding him. No one else moved. "I was the only one to come out," Pelowook said. "I think of all those passengers, all unconscious at that time." When his senses picked up the crackle of fire and the growing smell of smoke, he forced himself to action.

Releasing his seat belt, Pelowook staggered to his feet, searched around, and caught up a large piece of metal debris to shield himself from the growing blaze. Scrambling over people and rubble, he located an opening in the plane. Then systematically, in spite of the shock to his own body, Pelowook began pulling people from the wreckage, the closest ones first.

One . . . two, he dragged out. Three . . . four. On and on. In he stumbled and out again. He soon grew tired, one hand severely burned from holding the shield. The intense heat forced him back, but the flat metal kept the flames at bay while he freed yet another passenger. Eight . . . nine.

Growing weaker, ready to drop, Pelowook kept going. Each time he entered the opening, he had to stumble deeper into the plane to find passengers, deeper into the smoking inferno. An inner urgency drove him to speed, knowing any second the burning aircraft might explode, killing everyone—and himself—in a flash. Survivors outside began dragging themselves away from the wreckage.

Pelowook brought out more. Fifteen . . . sixteen. Totally exhausted now, the trooper would not give up. Eighteen . . . nineteen. Still he struggled on, until finally a series of explosions occurred. No hope remained for the rest of the victims.

Within a half hour of the crash, the villagers began arriving, out of breath from scrambling up the hill. By then fire blazed through the whole area.

One of the first at the wreck was retired public health nurse Corrine Kerfoot, who just happened to be visiting Gambell at the time. Her knowledge and experience took over, for she knew which injuries needed urgent attention. Kerfoot splinted broken bones and, with the other residents, applied first aid and organized the scene.

Before long, villagers—among them National Guard members—set up a steady evacuation down and around the cliff. Although Gambell proved only a half mile from the crash site in a direct line, villagers had to plod five miles around the cliff base in order to transport the injured out.

H. Vernon Slwooko Jr., who worked on the new Gambell housing, was one of the first on the scene. "We used some debris to bring the people back— some metal. We used some of the plane's structure for the wounded," he said.

Villagers then ferried the survivors across a small lake and carried them to the village school where an aid station had been prepared. A mood of hope mixed with despair hung over the scene, as rescuers comforted injured friends and relatives, and the grim job of identifying the victims began. Before long, the U.S. Coast Guard and a medical team from Nome arrived on site.

On Sunday morning pilots flew survivors to Anchorage medical facilities, where all the injured experienced slow but steady recovery. Most of the victims suffered from fractures, burns, and internal injuries. Pelowook arrived at a Nome hospital, where doctors treated him for a burned hand and released him. In all, ten on board died, including the pilot and copilot.

A member of the incoming medical team reported the front of the plane totally destroyed by fire. The remaining central section was wrecked, but fairly intact, and the wings folded over the top like some resting insect. Cause for the crash focused on the plane's flight recorder, equipment that linked cockpit and ground communications.

Authorities presented two State of Alaska Awards for Bravery-Heroism for courage and service during this disaster. One was granted to the people of Gambell, who gave up their personal possessions and their energies to aid the survivors. They were also commended for "taking them [survivors] from the crash site across difficult terrain to Gambell and caring for them until additional help arrived." By so doing, the residents of Gambell "averted further injury or death."

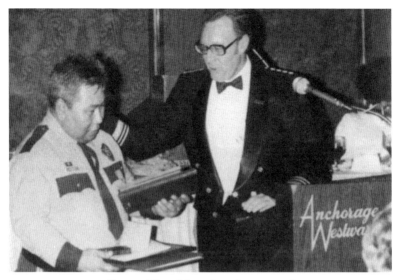

Trooper Gilbert Pelowook receives an award
from Commissioner Richard L. Burton in Anchorage, 1975.

Several officials recommended the medal for Pelowook. Norton Sound Health physician's assistant W. R. Bookhout said, "He freed himself, shook off his own injuries, and moved every passenger who survived off the aircraft before it burned." Bookhout then added, "A man of less will could not have shaken off his own injuries and moved as many people off the aircraft as he did without collapsing of sheer exhaustion, mental and physical."

John Reed, chairman of the National Transportation Safety Board, added his more formal comments: "Trooper Pelowook displayed a high degree of courage and bravery and is to be commended for his lifesaving actions."

In October 1975, Alaska State Trooper Gilbert Pelowook was scheduled to receive his medal, but bad weather in Nome prevented Governor Jay Hammond's flight to Savoonga. Not until December 4 did the governor make the formal presentation, personally, in Nome. Officials credited Pelowook with saving all twenty-two passengers who survived, at great risk to himself. In a letter to the trooper, Governor Hammond stated Pelowook joined a distinguished list of Alaskans "who have shown their love for their fellow man through individual unselfish actions, often at their own great personal risk."

More than ten years later, in October 1988, Gilbert Pelowook suffered his own disaster when his Savoonga residence burned down. Along with the contents, fire destroyed the Alaska medal and its certificates, awards more treasured by the trooper than his personal possessions. Pelowook's Nome lawyer wrote to then Governor Steve Cowper, stating, "The things Gilbert seems to miss the most are not adequately compensated by tort law." The Nome attorney made a plea to the governor's office, and the medal was replaced.

Gilbert Pelowook participated in other rescues before and after the Gambell disaster. A number of years later, irony played a hand in the trooper's life. In spite of his near-death experiences saving others in a variety of rescues, cancer took Pelowook's life in mid-June 1993. He passed away at the Alaska Native Hospital in Anchorage at the age of fifty-six. Pelowook's obituary, written by his niece, ended, "He will always be remembered with love in our hearts." He also lives on through the many people he saved, as well as their offspring. ★

# NO TURNING BACK

## Taku Inlet near Juneau, 1994

Not all sea emergencies occur under chaotic weather conditions—gale-force winds, freezing temperatures, giant waves. Sometimes the air is perfectly still with no wind at all, and the water is glassy.

Rain drizzled down on Juneau city early one calm Wednesday evening in June 1994. Mountains rimmed the Gastineau Channel, their snowcapped peaks obscured by low clouds and fog. The cruise ship SS *Universe*, docked in the harbor there, hosted hundreds of visitors from around the world. Among the passengers anxious to explore the Juneau area were retired vision and hearing specialist Wanda Gard and her friend, librarian Kathleen Pruneski—both from Michigan.

One of the options offered by the cruise social director was a flightseeing trip to Taku Glacier Lodge on Wings of Alaska floatplanes, about a thirty-mile trip by air southeast along Gastineau Channel and north following Taku Inlet. Inlet waters, washed down from Twin Glaciers, Hole-in-the-Wall Glacier, and several others, are extremely silty and cold.

According to a promotional flyer, the single-engine De Havilland Otter aircraft flew tourists "past lush green mountains with snow capped peaks . . . the awesome splendor of five glaciers, cascading waterfalls, and the beautiful Taku River Valley." While at the lodge, guests strolled around or enjoyed "the gourmet, alder-grilled king salmon feast and beverages chilled with glacier ice." An appealing experience for any sightseer. Many visitors reserving the three-hour outing considered it "the highlight" of their Alaskan adventure, and the *Universe* social director had no trouble booking a number of flights during the day.

Gard and Pruneski, excited by the adventure, signed on. Wings of Alaska pilots had mapped the trip within a comfortable time frame: the planes left downtown, flew to the lodge, landed passengers, reboarded others who had finished their stay, and returned to Juneau. From there planes turned around and flew back to the lodge, picking up remaining tourists. For this day, the airline scheduled flights every two hours or so, commencing at 8:00 A.M. Although the first trip was canceled due to weather, visibility cleared enough by 10:00 A.M. to begin shuttling passengers.

The Wings of Alaska boarding dock at the Juneau harbor.

An experienced pilot, Captain George Coulter, fifty-one, had worked a dozen years for Wings of Alaska and flown the flightseeing trip "several thousand times," according to company co-owner Bob Jacobsen. He piloted that Wednesday all day until early evening. When the final return began, Coulter took off with an empty plane from the Juneau dock, eventually setting down at the lodge by 7:00 P.M.

Taku Lodge, situated in the mountains, housed no weather reporting facilities, nor were there any along Taku River Inlet. For the evening in the vicinity, Juneau radio announced "mountains occasionally obscured in clouds and precipitation . . . occasional ceiling at or below one thousand feet with three to five miles visibility with light drizzle and fog." A wind would have cleared the air, but none materialized; stillness hung over the inlet, the waters calm, even mirrorlike. Evening light continued longer these hours, as it was the day after the summer solstice—the longest day of the year. Daylight lasted from 4:00 in the morning until 10:00 at night.

Visitors Gard and Pruneski enjoyed their stay at the lodge and noticed the fog patches. Before leaving, the group joked with resort owner Ken Ward: "If it gets too foggy, will you put us up for the night?"

When it came time to leave, Coulter boarded his ten-seat Otter. Besides Gard and Pruneski, other tourists included older couple Donald and Florence Schrantz from New York and Caroline Garner from Michigan. Also on board was a family from Guatemala consisting of elderly Margarette de Munoz, her friend Rose Marie Gomar de Vides, her daughter, Rosa, and Rosa's two children—Marie, seven, and Miguel, five.

On the original trip to the lodge, Rosa had flown copilot next to Coulter. Pruneski, always curious and ready for adventure, asked to occupy that front seat on the turnaround. No problem. Rosa, Gard, and the others settled in back.

Once loaded, five floatplanes took off—pilot Mike Olsen first, then Rusty Shaub, James Roe, Coulter fourth in line, and last Kevin Kramer—all flying with about two miles between planes. En route, Captain Olsen, the first to depart, alerted the other pilots by radio that "we needed to go from Flat Point to the vicinity between Turner Lake and Jaw Point, and that we may need to land due to the low ceilings." Three pilots ahead set up their planes for landing on the water because of the fog, but the weather improved as they flew on, and the Otters continued the routine flight to Juneau.

According to Coulter's passenger Margarette de Munoz, weather was good when they took off from the lodge: "They tried to fly over the glacier but couldn't get over the glacier, so they flew towards the river and descended."

Weather in Coulter's area—scattered fog layers—deteriorated as he traveled downriver toward Scow Cove. He chose to navigate Taku Inlet to the east side as the other aircraft had done. Coulter did not enter the clouds, and he later stated he had at least two miles of visibility at all times. As he made the crossing, he lost sight of the shoreline. Passenger Gard said she could not see out of the aircraft more than ten feet because of fog. Coulter decided to touch down on the river and began losing altitude.

Landing on glassy water proves difficult because it affects a pilot's depth perception. "It's like landing on a mirror," Wings of Alaska co-owner Bob Jacobsen explained. "You have no accurate sense of how far above the water surface you are due to the type of light, the mist in the air, and the grayness of the river water." A pilot needs tree height, waves, debris—something—to get a fix on the surface.

Pilot Coulter glided down for a landing. He reported to the National Transportation Safety Board that he "last recalled seeing the altimeter at two hundred feet indicated, and just as the Turner Lake shoreline came into view the airplane struck the water." Since the crash occurred with no warning, no distress call went out.

When the Otter hit, the impact smashed out the front window, the engine split off the plane due to water ingestion, then the motor careened under the aircraft, chopping holes in the floats. Water flooded in the front, washing down the aisle toward the tail.

"Put on your life jackets!" Coulter called through the chaos. "Get out the rear doors." He tried slipping on his life preserver, but his fingers wouldn't work right. "Get out!" he kept shouting.

"The door—it's jammed!" someone cried.

Coulter hiked up out the broken front window, ran across the top of the aircraft toward the tail. From above, he reached down and jerked the handle of the left door and pulled it open. Then he dove over the other side and, with feet against the airplane, jerked on the right door. With a super strength only urgency seems to provide, he ripped the door off.

No sooner had the plane hit than Gard snapped up her life preserver. She seized another one, thinking to give it to her friend, and started fighting her way forward.

"I saw water about waist high coming down the aisle," she said. "I grabbed a second life preserver and wanted to take it to Kathy, but other passengers in the front of the plane, as well as packages, were coming down the aisle towards me. I couldn't get through."

She struggled out a back door instead and jumped into the glacial water, bitterly cold. The aircraft went down fast and left people drifting in the icy river—Gard counted six survivors. Once outside floating on the surface, catching her breath, she looked around for her friend, but could not see her. Noticing the little girl nearby with no life vest, Gard passed the extra preserver over and told her to hang on.

Somehow, Gard did not focus on the cold. She didn't want to die, so she told herself, "If I want to live, I have to help myself. I have to save my strength." Glancing around, she spotted two pieces of wreckage—one cone-shaped that did not look buoyant, and another like a pontoon. That was better. In spite of the weakness coming over her, Gard swam a short distance, tired, floated, swam again, tired, floated, until she made the piece of debris. There she hung on.

A distance away, Coulter bobbed on the surface. "Get together," he yelled, realizing some had no life vests on.

Rosa Gomar de Vides, mother of young Miguel and Maria, held on to a floating door with the children. "Stay there," Coulter ordered. He spotted a bow section of the plane drifting about a hundred feet away and swam for that, thinking he could bring it back. But the shock, the glacial thirty- to forty-degree Fahrenheit water, sapped his strength. He slowed and started to sink.

A voice in his head shouted, NO! forcing him to struggle up. Gard saw him making his way toward her. "Come on, George," she yelled. Coulter willed himself to stay on top and barely made the float himself. He and Gard both clung to the floating wreckage. "Hold on!" Coulter kept shouting to everyone.

With no life vest, Rosa's little boy finally "fell asleep," let go of the floating door, and drifted away. During that time, the survivors said they saw someone float by. In their shocked, hypothermic state, however, they felt bewildered, helpless.

"After we were in the water for about fifteen minutes," stated Rosa Gomar de Vides, "the fog became so thick that I could not see anything." Her ear caught a voice asking the pilot what had happened, and she heard someone respond, "It was too foggy and I was flying too low."

Gard, too numb to question what was happening to her, hung on to her piece of debris for her very life. "I tried to move my body, thinking it might help to keep me warm, but I soon felt tingling . . . and shivering beyond my control . . . then I rested, thinking this is the end for me, and I was going to die. Next I saw what looked like twinkling stars and passed out."

No human witnessed the accident. However, an Alaska Electric Light and Power Company employee, Dick Emberton, stationed at the Annex Creek hydroelectric plant near Scow Cove, reported, "I heard the Otters going by, and I thought, 'God, it's kind of bad for those guys to be flying out there.'" He said the weather had been poor for some time. After hearing the crash noise, he called and discussed the possibilities with another employee; the two decided it probably was not one of the planes anyway.

There, about a mile or so away from the power plant, each victim bobbed on the calm surface, in the middle of a wilderness glacial river, water survival time estimated at ninety minutes maximum. No sound or action in the air distracted them from their grim thoughts as the cold numbed them, drained them of their warmth, confused them, and robbed them of their will to live. Eventually all of them drifted in and out of consciousness.

Since the trip back to Juneau for the other floatplanes was routine, nobody thought of Coulter. No problem had worried the pilots coming in, and they believed the fifth pilot flew close behind. Only after the other four planes touched down and unloaded their passengers was Coulter's airplane missed. With no word from the Otter, immediately three aircraft did a turnaround, took off, and headed back to Taku Inlet. The pilot of the fourth plane suspected mechanical trouble on his Otter and remained behind.

The Wings of Alaska's downtown Juneau office, above their plane docking facilities.

By returning to Taku Inlet, the three pilots backtracked into the conditions that had jeopardized them in the first place, the very weather that might have downed their colleague—if that was the case. Layered fog still hung over the area, and the weather deteriorated.

At the same time, officials alerted the U.S. Coast Guard, which dispatched the 110-foot cutter *Liberty* from Juneau and a helicopter from Sitka. An Alaska Fish and Wildlife ship, the *Enforcer*, also sped out. Other air and water units, both private and agency, responded. Captain Olsen radioed ahead to Ken Ward at Taku Glacier Lodge asking him to run a skiff down the river to check from that direction.

Pilots Kramer and Shaub finally landed on the calm, flat Taku Inlet water and taxied around until they located a fuel sheen. When Olsen reached the scene, he said patchy fog prevailed. He flew low once, spotted nothing, and went up again. Finally the pilot sighted several survivors and scattered debris on the water, gathered in a riptide. From what he could tell, he saw no sign of the children. Olsen notified the other search units and glided in.

With the fog as heavy as it was, it amazed Coulter in the river that Olsen found them at all. Coulter remembered seeing Olsen's landed Otter easing through the mist like a materializing ghost, slowly sliding toward him, gently bumping him in the water. "He was led by God" was the only answer Coulter could find.

From the rescue Otter, Olsen struggled to lift the soaked Coulter into the plane, eventually succeeding. Then he grabbed a paddle and reached Gard, who wore a life vest. But by then his strength was gone, and she proved too numb to help. Olsen held on to her, talking to her, keeping her awake. Ken Ward of Taku Glacier Lodge arrived by skiff with two others soon after and helped lift Gard into the Otter.

After that Ward discovered the small body of seven-year-old Marie, which had been floating face down in the icy water for a long time. Later rescuers located a woman's body, believed to be Florence Schrantz; Coast Guard crew transferred both victims to the Coast Guard's twenty-five-foot utility boat, which carried them to Juneau.

Captain Kevin Kramer kept busy himself, hoisting Margarette de Munoz into his floatplane. When pilot Rusty Shaub arrived, he saved Donald Schrantz and Rosa Gomar de Vides.

Without delay, the three aircraft sped the survivors back to Juneau. There ambulances rushed them to Bartlett Memorial Hospital, where doctors treated them for hypothermia. Soon after being admitted, Donald Schrantz passed away. Margarette de Munoz, Rosa Gomar de Vides, Wanda Gard, and pilot George Coulter pulled through.

Gard remembered waking in the hospital, hearing snatches of conversations, being examined. People came in to ask questions. She fell asleep again, and next she awoke in the intensive care unit.

Meanwhile, U.S. Coast Guard spokesman Lieutenant Ray Massey reported the fog at the site had worsened. Because of this the helicopter from Sitka plus several local aircraft could not search. "It was so bad . . . we couldn't even get our helicopter in there," reported Massey. "The crewman on our rescue boat had to sit on the bow to look around. He said he couldn't see his hand in front of his face." Boat units searched all night.

Wings' president, Bob Jacobsen spent hours at the hospital, talking with the survivors and doing what he could. A conversation with the mother of the children, Rosa, stayed with Jacobsen and gave him strength. After he apologized to her, she said, "It wasn't you who took my children, it was God. And now, my children are playing with God."

Wings of Alaska staff knew it was important to bring closure for family members after an ordeal like this. Thinking several bodies might still be in the wrecked plane, the next day Wings and the Alaska State Troopers arranged to send units to Flat Point for salvage operations. Errol Champion of Juneau lent his boat and sonar equipment to help ferret out the wreckage underwater.

On Friday swimmers from Commercial Diving Services prepared to plunge in and try to locate the downed Otter. Since glacier waters surge through the inlet, the passage flows as a murky, silty waterway, heavy with sandy particles. Divers cannot see debris. They have to first practice on land, with eyes covered, to recognize the contours of a plane by touch so they know what to feel for underwater. Ultimately divers jumped in and discovered zero visibility on the bottom.

"It was like wrapping a towel around your head three times," one diver said. Even with bright lights, "you couldn't see anything."

"Besides the problem of working in water, salvaging presented other dangers," said diver Peter Lind. "First, you couldn't see anything. Then, with a crashed plane, your breathing equipment, your personal or motorized equipment, could get hung up on broken pieces. Not to mention the terrific currents running through there."

Lieutenant Robin Lown, spokesman for the troopers, remarked, "If divers determine it is too hazardous, they may try 'grappling' for the wreckage by lowering large hooks and trying to snag it." In the end, that's what they did. After laboring for hours, workers sent a line down and hooked something at about ninety feet. Underwater currents, however, wriggled it free.

Salvage operations continued over the weekend in spite of a turn in the weather. Winds in Taku Inlet whipped the glassy waters into wild seas—making a delicate job nearly impossible. Rescue crews repeatedly dropped a line to hook the plane. "Strong tidal and river currents are making it difficult to snag the wreckage and winch it along to shallow, clearer water," Rusty Shaub reported.

On Tuesday the diving crew finally succeeded in hooking the Otter and pulling it into seventeen feet of water. At that point workers attached more lines and dragged it to the beach. Eventually three bodies—those of Pruneski, Garner, and the older Gomar de Vides woman—were freed from the wreckage and flown to Juneau.

Employees of Wings of Alaska had trouble dealing with the disaster. Jacobsen arranged for counselors to talk with Wings' staff directly involved, and their families. The following Thursday the company canceled all flightseeing trips for the day. "Company employees are grieving the first fatal accident in Wings' almost twelve-year history," the chief pilot said.

The Gomar de Vides family flew to Juneau from Guatemala to be with the relatives and grieve together. Realizing a religious gathering would support the survivors, Catholic Bishop Michael Kenny said and sang a Mass for the victims

Wanda Gard and former Wings of Alaska pilot Mike Olsen, who took Wanda to the site of the disaster several years later—on a calm, beautiful day in 1997.

and their families—in fluent Spanish. "It was a therapeutic gathering and a meaningful celebration for the lives lost," said Jacobsen.

Wanda Gard revived in the next few days. Curious to know what her temperature registered when brought to the hospital, a nurse replied: 83.5 degrees Fahrenheit. Wings of Alaska flew her son Larry to Juneau, and he took her to Michigan on Saturday. With bruises and aggravated arthritis from the cold, she mended back home.

Because of the four pilots' selfless rescue work in extreme weather, Mike Olsen, Rusty Shaub, and Kevin Kramer were awarded the State of Alaska Award for Bravery-Heroism in December of 1994 by Governor Walter Hickel, who praised their bravery and humane actions. George Coulter received his medal at the same time for his "great bravery and tremendous presence of mind under the most stressful of circumstances."

Pride in the heroism award mixed with reservations as aviation agencies investigated the accident. After some legalities, authorities revoked George Coulter's pilot's license for several months during the inquiry. Eventually he was found not guilty of any wrongdoing. Probable cause of the accident, according to aviation safety officials: failure to maintain altitude above the river due to adverse weather and the glassy surface of the water. The tragedy, after thirty-five years of flying, left a sour taste in Coulter's mouth, and he retired. Occasionally he still has bad dreams about the accident.

The aftermath of this tragedy still lives with those involved. Olsen, a new father at the time, said the accident helped him decide against flying—in favor of a land job. Shaub remained a pilot, as did Kramer. Speaking of the disaster, "It's something that happened in your life, and you do what anyone would do," Kramer summed it up. "Yet, you never want to repeat the experience."

Once returned to Michigan, Gard attended Pruneski's funeral on July 5, and through the months mourned her friend. A social worker suggested grief counseling, which helped Gard come to grips with the death. Gard has not been up in a small plane since the accident, and although flying makes her nervous, she has no problem with larger jets.

A couple of years later Gard returned to Juneau with some of her family. She requested to see the site of the crash, and Olsen took her on his boat to the scene. The weather cooperated with calm, sunny skies, and Gard felt a kind of closure then. The setting—the beautiful mountains, the wildness—framed the kind of backdrop Pruneski loved. It would have satisfied her sense of adventure. Gard said of her friend's death, "I believe if she had had a choice, it would have been someplace like this."

The body of five-year-old Miguel Gomar de Vides has never been found. ★

★

# DOING IT THE HARD WAY

## Nome, 1993

Nothing but best wishes traveled with twenty-five members of the Fellowship Ministries headed to eastern Russia in August 1993. Pastor Dave Anderson, headquartered in Tempe, Arizona, had organized a group of gospel musicians from Alaska and other states to lead the calling—the "Siberian Mission" he named it. Besides gospel entertainment, they delivered medical supplies, food, and Bibles to the people of Lavrentiya, Russia. After three days of meetings there, the group prepared to return to Nome via Provideniya, Russia.

Everyone, of course, expected a routine flight.

David Cochran, veteran pilot of Missionary Aviation Repair Center (MARC) of Kenai, piloted the first of four MARC planes returning to Alaska from Russia after completing the church mission. The aircraft he operated, a beige, 1974 twin-engine Piper Navajo, could carry eleven people, but only six passengers and pilot Cochran boarded. The party included Alaska resident Pam Swedberg, Soldotna; Barbara and David Anderson, Arizona; Cary Dietsche, Wisconsin; Brian Brasher, Illinois; and Donald Wharton, Tennessee.

The fact that it was Friday the thirteenth did not deter the missionaries. Once readied, the plane lifted from Provideniya with enough fuel for the 375-mile flight to Nome. Russian airport fuel supplies were so scarce, MARC expected to shuttle gas back to Provideniya for the other three missionary planes waiting to return. In fact, Cochran carried twenty empty plastic blue and white five-gallon gas jugs for that purpose.

The flight plan called for a stop in Gambell, Saint Lawrence Island, for refueling and clearing U.S. Customs. In Gambell, however, Cochran learned fuel was unavailable. Figuring he could make it with what gas remained, he flew the Piper Navajo skyward in the late afternoon to continue the remainder of the two-hundred-mile journey to Nome.

Less than an hour later, closing in on the mainland toward Nome, Cochran checked his fuel gauge and his map, and realized they would never make it. He decided to try for a beach landing on Sledge Island, about five miles off the Alaska mainland and twenty-five miles west of Nome. As he eventually viewed Sledge Island in the distance, however, Cochran realized even that was too far. Radioing Nome Flight Service, he transmitted his position and requested help.

Nome: "November Six Sierra Foxtrot, are you declaring an emergency?"

Cochran: "Yes . . . please. I'm about two miles short of Sledge Island."

Nome: "Say how many souls on board."

Cochran: "Seven."

Soon after, the pilot alerted the passengers they would have to ditch; the plane began to lose altitude.

Passenger Pam Swedberg thought of her husband. He piloted planes out of Soldotna, so when the Piper Navajo's first engine went out, Pam remembered her husband practicing with one engine and did not panic. After the second engine coughed and sputtered, she knew they were going down. She grabbed an empty gas jug, jammed it between her knees, and assumed a crash position.

Lower and lower the Navajo descended. Missionary Cary Dietsche, sitting in front, gripped the front door latch, watched the water seemingly reach up for the plane. He couldn't help thinking of his wife and kids back in Wisconsin. Would he ever see them again? He didn't want to die, and his strong faith helped calm his fears. Glancing around, he saw Donald Wharton grab the back emergency door handle. They exchanged eye signals, ready for action when the plane hit.

As smoothly as possible, to keep the Piper Navajo from breaking up, pilot Cochran eased the plane down at ninety miles per hour and belly flopped it on the surface. One wing caught a three-foot wave and swung the aircraft around.

With the jolting landing, Dietsche shot backward and found himself still belted in, seat and all, in the rear of the plane. The emergency door had burst open and flown off, sucking out a number of empty gas jugs. The front door popped free too, and Dietsche remembered climbing over a jumble of luggage to get to it while others scrambled out the emergency exit. As passengers ditched the plane into the forty-five-degree Fahrenheit seas, one member passed out empty fuel jugs for flotation.

Swedberg jumped into the ocean first, the icy shock taking her breath away. Barbara Anderson followed, then others. Within moments, the Piper Navajo sank. Alone, practically invisible, the seven drifted in heavy, sodden clothing in the numbing waters, losing strength and body heat with every second, wondering if anyone even knew they were down.

Earlier, Bering Air pilot Terry Day had taken off from the Gambell landing strip at about the same time as the missionary plane. He was an hour behind schedule and hurried to make up time. Day made a short hop to Savoonga just

This closeup shows the rocky shoreline of small Sledge Island.

before the missionaries began their trip and then flew on a direct route to Nome with two passengers. As he neared Sledge Island southwest of Nome, he "happened to see a splash" out of the corner of his eye. "I thought it was a whale," he went on to say, "because it was about ten or fifteen miles away."

Minutes later, Nome headquarters asked Day to detour to Sledge Island and look around; a plane was having trouble, the flight center said, and planned to land on the beach there.

Day then realized what he had seen: "A light bulb went off in my head, and I said, 'I'll bet you that's what that splash was that I had seen five to eight minutes earlier.'"

Immediately, Day diverted to the splash area. Back and forth he flew, peering down at the choppy water. Five minutes, ten minutes, time eating his fuel. At last he caught sight of something . . . yes! With no orange life vests or preservers, no raft, the survivors bobbed like bits of seaweed on the water—very difficult to locate. Day notified Nome to send out a helicopter right away.

Despite his fuel gauge registering nearly empty, Day continued circling the scene, afraid others might not find the victims otherwise. "They were really, really hard to spot," he said.

Another small plane flown by Vic Olson of Baker Aviation overheard the emergency call and sidetracked to the scene from a Shishmaref trip. While Day banked, hurrying to Nome, Olson took over his position above the survivors until the expected helicopter arrived.

Down below in the icy sea, the missionaries rode on three- to four-foot waves, their bodies weakening with every roll. A few of them splashed and waved to the pilot; others couldn't summon the energy.

Relief sent a spark of hope through Swedberg on seeing the plane circling overhead but, because it was a wheeled aircraft, she understood it could not land. She also knew, sensing her own weakness, that hypothermia drained heat from everyone's body with each passing second. Minute after minute she asked herself how long could they all last until a floatplane or a helicopter arrived. She blacked out once, and on coming aware again got a grip on herself: "You can't do this," she said in her head. "They are coming," she kept repeating, willing herself to be saved.

While in Nome, Eric Pentilla, pilot for Evergreen Helicopters, pushed his chair back after finishing dinner, thoughts of a little late fishing running through his mind. He reached the outside door as the rescue call from Nome Flight Service came in. Pentilla headed for the hangar, picking up his mechanic, Jerry Austin, along with the "strongest, biggest" firefighter he could locate—Randy Oles. Within a half hour, Pentilla's chopper lifted from the airfield for the twenty-minute flight to Sledge Island.

About the same time, Era helicopter pilot Walt Greaves was flying technician Dave Miles over portions of the mainland doing an electromagnetic survey for a Canadian corporation. He caught the call for assistance from the Nome Flight Service and radioed Pentilla. "I want you over here now," Pentilla said. "I'm going to need help." Greaves and his companion ditched the geology equipment on a mountaintop, wheeled the helicopter around, and sped toward Sledge Island.

When pilot Pentilla arrived on the scene, he spotted only six of the seven survivors in the sea. His helicopter was equipped with landing skids, not floats, so he could not totally set down on the surface, but had to hover over it. To rescue, he had to dip a skid into the water while Oles helped pull the victims out.

Taking the helicopter down, Pentilla found pickup difficult with the chopper blades spraying water in the missionaries' faces. On the other hand, he noticed with relief the empty jugs keeping the victims afloat. He began the operation.

For Pentilla, a veteran pilot of more than twenty years, this was his first rescue picking live people out of the water. True, he had once plucked a person from the sea with a rope and tire, but most of his rescue work, sadly enough, involved dead bodies.

Pentilla, however, knew what to do. Sitting on the right side of the chopper, he constantly glanced left for any large rogue wave that might swamp the operation. Because he could not fully see Oles on the skid blade, Austin wore a headset inside the helicopter cabin and relayed information as to what was going on at the surface.

Rescuers positioned themselves to take missionary Brian Brasher first. However, he pointed to Dietsche, who was having back and leg problems after the crash—plus his fingers were so cramped from the cold, he could no longer hold on to the floating jug. Fireman Oles in an orange survival suit straddled the skid and literally dragged and pushed Dietsche out of the water, while Austin pulled the survivor into the cabin. With a ninety-minute survival clock ticking in these freezing waters, already half had been used up by the time this first rescue occurred.

Missionary Dave Anderson was next. With Anderson's strength gone, and his clothing soaked, only after he managed to hike his leg over the skid did rescuers pull him in. By then, hypothermia gripped both Dietsche and Anderson, and they hardly moved.

Rescuers had more difficulty hauling pilot Cochran in. A heavy, soaking wet parka dragged his body down. He floated stiffly and nearly unconscious, both arms rigidly outstretched, which made him difficult to maneuver. Cochran later recalled those moments. "I just waited it out. There's nothing you could do. There's no way to swim; you'd just burn up too much energy."

Finally, Cochran lost consciousness entirely, and rescuers thought he was dead. "One minute he'd be right at the skid and ready to go," Austin said, "and the next minute a three-foot swell would come and he'd drop down every time they'd get hold of him." Many times Cochran sank underwater until they hauled him up. Since they could not heft the MARC pilot into the aircraft, they wrapped a rope around him and secured him as best they could, draped over the skid.

Oles and Austin were so tired by then, Pentilla knew they would never get the MARC pilot into the plane. He called his intentions to the two rescuers. Then pilot Pentilla slowly lifted the helicopter into the air and headed for Sledge Island, while Oles and Austin struggled, riding and physically holding Cochran over the narrow skid. Though survivors inside the aircraft—Anderson and Dietsche—were too weak to help much, they held on to a rope wrapped around Cochran outside. This added some support and heft to the rescuers holding on the skid.

With no level or safe spot to land near the rocky beach, Pentilla began swooping to a seven-hundred-foot cleared plateau high on Sledge Island, about the height of a sixty-story building. Each man wondered if Cochran was still alive, whether they would make it, whether Cochran would slip off, falling from a deadly height onto the rocky shore far below.

Closer and closer the chopper swung up, up, the men watching, holding their breath, until at last they made it to the top. Once settled on the plateau, Pentilla threw a dry sleeping bag over the MARC pilot, again climbed into the helicopter, and hurried back out for more missionaries. Speed proved important. The rescuers figured those left in the icy sea would not last much longer.

Three crash victims out of the water now, four more to go.

By that time, pilot Greaves had arrived with his Era helicopter, hovering over the water. Dave Miles, the geology engineer with him, opened the door and tried to haul a woman—Barbara Anderson—into the helicopter. With her bulky clothing totally soaked, the weight was too heavy to pull up. And as with Cochran's rescue, the constantly pitching three-foot waves also made positioning of the helicopter difficult. When a wave rode up, Anderson was within reach, but when it rolled down, the helicopter could not follow for fear the tail rotor would catch the wave and cause a disaster.

While geologist Miles hung on to the skid with one hand, he tried to grab Anderson on the up swell with his other hand—she too weak to help. There proved no way, with leverage or strength, that he could pull her into the aircraft by himself. Yet he knew he had to haul her out of the freezing water or she would die.

When nothing worked, Miles, held by a seat belt, clasped the woman with his knees between her head and shoulders and wrapped his legs around her chest. He then signaled Greaves to take off. As they gained altitude, the uplift literally plucked Anderson from the water as they flew toward the island. Almost there, she, dangling, waterlogged, began slipping, Miles losing his grip. He cried out to Greaves—they couldn't fly high to the plateau; she might slip off and plunge to her death. One hundred feet from shore, Greaves cut altitude, lowering the chopper about ten feet above the sea, and the missionary slipped off, falling. This time Anderson, totally numb, drifted in water with no floating gas jug holding her up.

Greaves swooped to shore, dropping Miles to the ground. The geologist fumbled over slippery rocks, at last stumbling back into the water to pick up Anderson. It took some struggling by stages to pull her in and help her over

Cary Dietsche gets an assist from Kevin Ahl and Randy Oles.

the rocks onto the beach, but they finally arrived. Miles said she was happy to be on land again.

Three more missionaries to go.

Meanwhile, pilot Pentilla and Oles circled back to the site to rescue Pam Swedberg. Oles threw a line to her, pulled her toward the chopper, and tried to hoist her up, again and again. Not until Swedberg managed to lift a knee to the skid for support did Oles obtain enough leverage to heft her out and pack her into the aircraft. There she sat, numbly thinking this was her first helicopter ride and wishing circumstances were different; she wanted to sit in the cockpit and really enjoy it.

The next missionary to be saved was Donald Wharton, "a really big guy" wearing a snowmachine suit. When they could not lift him into the aircraft, Oles remained on the skid with him, and Austin spread out on the floor inside the helicopter. He reached forward outside and held on to them both as the helicopter flew toward land. Another dangerous trip, but they made it to the top of Sledge Island.

With survival time running out and Pentilla busy, Walt Greaves made hopeless swings over the water trying to spot the last missionary, Brian Brasher. Greaves, thinking Brasher would be in the general area with the others, overflew a six-hundred-foot sweep scattered with the floating gas jugs, but sun shining on the water made it hard to see. Brasher had given up his chance at rescue during the beginning of the mission—was he then the one to be lost forever?

Down below in the ocean, gas can gripped under the surface, Brasher lost heart. He could see the plane, but there was no way to signal. And when Greaves, alone in the chopper, overflew him four times, Brasher grew desperate. Floating in the icy waters for seventy minutes, Brasher was about to pack it in.

Finally Greaves spotted him. Since he could not complete the rescue, being alone, Greaves radioed ahead and hovered over Brasher until Pentilla and his team flew out and fished Brasher out. Pentilla radioed Nome to have medical aid ready.

After picking up Barbara Anderson and Dave Miles at the foot of Sledge Island, Pentilla flew them with Brasher to the island's plateau, where the others gathered. Pentilla then took four on his helicopter, Greaves loaded the remaining three, and both choppers sped to the Nome airfield. The fire department and ambulances waited there to whisk survivors to the Norton Sound Hospital, where a medical team treated them for hypothermia. With warmth and care, all the missionaries recovered in good shape in spite of their seventy-minute ordeal in near-freezing water.

Survivor David Anderson from Phoenix said, "Those barrels [jugs] were absolute lifesavers. We could not have stayed in the water that long without hanging on to the barrels." That fact proved particularly important since the airplane did not carry life vests for the passengers.

After the missionaries healed in the hospital, Alaska Airlines flew them—first class—to Anchorage. On the trip out of Nome the pilot sidetracked and banked over Sledge Island so the survivors could have a last glance at their recovery site.

Many of the Sledge Island rescuers and rescued, plus a few FAA personnel.

Following this rescue, Pentilla and Oles tailored a three-piece safety device, much like a parachute harness, that can secure a person to a helicopter exterior during a rescue.

Days afterward, Oles said he was so pumped up he had trouble sleeping as well as recalling some details of the rescue. One forgotten memory was catching sight of a miliary aircraft that flew overhead during the rescue. They could have dropped a raft if signaled to do so, but the pilots had landed most of the victims by then, and little time remained.

Pilot Day, who originally spotted the seven off Sledge Island, thought the missionaries truly fortunate. "There were too many variables that all fell into place," he said. "Call it divine intervention." He then went on to speak of the lack of rescue facilities in Nome. "There is nobody here in town set up for emergency rescues. These people are extremely, extremely lucky to have been found. These people came in a hairbreadth of dying."

For their unselfish courage in saving the missionaries, authorities flew Pentilla, Greaves, Oles, and Austin to Juneau, Alaska, to receive the State of Alaska Award for Bravery-Heroism, presented by Governor Walter Hickel in November 1994.

"The people of Alaska are a hearty bunch who are known for their willingness to come to the aid of others in difficulty. As governor, it is a privilege to be able to recognize you for your great Alaskan spirit," Hickel praised.

Other awards were also forthcoming, notably one from the director of the Federal Aviation Administration in Washington, D.C., David Hinson, who traveled to Nome to make presentations.

Missionary Dietsche, a worship and music director for his church in Wisconsin, occasionally still thinks about that traumatic time. He becomes a little anxious about flying, still has back problems, but is thankful for each day with his family. Other missionaries also have returned to their U.S. homes, grateful for their survival. Dave Cochran has retired and no longer flies.

Once home in Soldotna after the crash, Pam Swedberg experienced a recurring dream—simply that she was underwater with her hand above the surface. The dream has faded, and Swedberg has taken up a more grounded life now. Flying does not figure as intensely—she raises a family, no longer flies on gospel missions, and is somewhat nervous about lifting off in small planes, while her husband changed jobs from flying to construction. Pam remains a strong church member.

Five years after the ordeal, several of the missionaries and their rescuers returned to Nome for a reunion. All those involved—from nurses to flight controllers—joined in the celebration.

Helicopter pilot Pentilla expressed his personal feelings: "We are always happy when we have a happy ending like this. A lot of times when I get called out, it's a fatality. Very seldom do we get to go out and save lives like we did, so that's a pretty good feeling."

Carrying very little emergency equipment, the rescuers used experience and any method they could to save the missionaries. Pentilla had flown out to Sledge Island on that August day prepared with several emergency articles he never had to use. His excess emergency items? Seven body bags. ★

★

# IT'S NOW OR NEVER

## Cordova, 1983

For all the spectacular scenery and superior days in Alaska, the weather can turn truly nasty. Storms sweeping north across the vast Gulf of Alaska rake the Southcentral region with relentless force. Thus continued a blizzard in the northern gulf on January 13, 1983—the dead of winter.

Flying for Kennedy Air Service, pilot Gayle Ranney followed a western course returning to Cordova in a single-engine Cessna 185 after dropping a passenger off at Cape Yakataga. Below, the eastern run of the Copper River drained into a braided delta expanse. For miles, an isolated wilderness of mountains and glaciers backed sandbars and tidal flats fronting the gulf.

On that Thursday, winds gusting to hurricane force scoured the Copper River delta region, with sudden snow squalls sheeting down, causing whiteout conditions. The long winter nights and dark days opened only a short window of daylight.

Weather forced Ranney to land her ski-equipped plane on a frozen riverbank near Softuk Bar, about four miles west of the abandoned town of Katalla. The wind-jostled landing knocked off Ranney's landing gear and caused some damage to her propeller. She was uninjured. When she later tried to take off, a ski broke, thus stranding her.

Ranney flashed an emergency call to the nearest town, Cordova. Equipped with sleeping bag and supplies, she settled down and waited for help.

Due to weather and terrain, Ranney's emergency transmission did not get through. By chance, an Alaska Airlines jet high overhead heard the emergency locator transponder (ELT) and radioed the signal to the Federal Aviation Administration (FAA) in Cordova. Immediately rescue wheels began turning. Besides launching a hunt by air, officials alerted twenty-five Cordova fire and police volunteers in case circumstances called for a ground search.

In Cordova, Alaska Fish and Wildlife protection officers also served as state troopers. Officer John Stimson, skipper of the Fish and Wildlife patrol vessel *Enforcer*, heard of the downed plane. With years of experience in law enforcement, Stimson pinpointed time as the priority and immediately chartered a Chisum Flying Service Bell Jet Ranger helicopter. Chisum pilot Gary Wiltrout had been flying supplies west of Cordova, back and forth to Cape Hinchinbrook Lighthouse that morning. Weather in that direction then was not good, but flyable.

Normally Stimson might have assigned one of his other three officers to assist with the rescue. However, one was sick, another on vacation, and the last rehearsing for a wedding—no one else was available. When Gary Wiltrout returned to base after his Hinchinbrook run, Stimson offered to help, and fly on the rescue mission. A short time later, the weather in Cordova eased slightly. Stimson and Wiltrout, anxious to get airborne and reach Ranney before the weather deteriorated, took off from Cordova about 1:30 in the afternoon.

Wiltrout's helicopter traced the Copper River Highway, crossing glaciers and rivers in the delta area. They veered off the highway at Mile 27 and headed south on their own. After notifying the FAA in Cordova, Wiltrout continued zeroing in on Ranney's emergency beacon signal.

Once Wiltrout's helicopter traveled over the Copper River, there was trouble. He knew flying at one hundred feet or higher over the water was all right. Lower, over land, the wind screamed in a funnel through the flats. But in order to see anything, and possibly pick up Ranney's ELT signal, conditions forced the plane to fly low, and Wiltrout tried to keep control. He estimated winds from seventy to ninety miles an hour, bearing heavy snow. Time, too, carried an urgency, for they lost daylight with each minute ticking by.

As the pilot approached a frozen river, he encountered total whiteout with fog and blowing snow. The aircraft began descending, with Wiltrout fighting to correct. But he couldn't see, and the aircraft kept pressing down. He managed a "Mayday" just before the helicopter nosed down, crashing on the left and rolling over.

At about 2:00 P.M. employees, including part-owner Petie Chisum, gathered in the Chisum Flying Service flight control office, keeping tabs on the weather and half listening to several radio channels. Used to the jumble of FAA news crackling over the airways, they suddenly stopped talking, stunned, when Wiltrout's familiar call letters broke through, followed by "Mayday, Mayday, Mayday. Engine failure." The airway went dead.

Stimson's wife, Trish, heard the "Mayday" over her single-sideband radio at home. She knew John would help coordinate the search from the office and wondered which of John's colleagues had been on the downed helicopter. They were all friends, and she was concerned—what could she do to help? And with a rescue in progress, she figured John would probably be late for dinner—what could she fix that would hold over?

A short time later, the office notified Trish: John, her husband, had accompanied Wiltrout on the rescue; it was he who had crashed with the helicopter. They had no further word. The news sent Trish hurrying to headquarters.

By then officials had alerted Air Force and Coast Guard rescue centers, and flights converged on Cordova from Anchorage and Kodiak. When the HC-130 communications aircraft from Elmendorf Air Force Base arrived at the Cordova airstrip, daylight had faded, and the weather worsened.

As light dimmed to late afternoon, Gayle Ranney on her isolated sandbar knew rescue efforts would not reach her that day. Although she did not pack much survival gear, she camped as best she could, hoping help would reach her the following day. The one wing of her Cessna buried in snow kept the aircraft from blowing away, and she planned to run the plane's engine periodically during the night to keep warm. Ranney had no idea that Wiltrout's helicopter had crashed only two miles from her location.

Because the helicopter and the Cessna were down so close to each other, rescuers had difficulty zeroing in on the emergency locator beacon; they could not tell which site emitted the signal.

Back at the Cordova command center, rescue crews worried about the downed men. They knew the baggage compartment in Wiltrout's helicopter carried plenty of survival gear—four sleeping bags and food rations for seven days. No problem there. The victims had a good chance for survival.

Nevertheless, wildlife officers in Cordova felt anxious and frustrated. Finally two drove the highway with a policeman on the chance the helicopter had gone down close to the road. Weather was no better by land. The icy highway proved useless; the powerful wind slid the four-wheel-drive pickup backward. Whiteout conditions also prevented snowmachine rescuers from searching at ground level. They planned on leaving the highway at Mile 27 for a river search, but weather halted their operations.

The helicopter accident in fact offered little hope for the two survivors— Wiltrout and Stimson. The impact had smashed out the cockpit's Plexiglas windows and compressed the machine like an accordion. Fortunately, the aircraft did not burn. Although the air blew bitter with a wind chill below minus fifty, the machine offered some protection.

Worst of all, the crash broke pilot Wiltrout's back, which made it impossible for him to move with any freedom. Stimson, himself weak, carefully dragged Wiltrout to the sheltered side of the ruined aircraft. Then Stimson repeatedly tried to recover survival gear from inside the wreckage.

On the Ranger, however, the baggage hold and the survival gear were stored on the left side of the aircraft. And when the helicopter went down, it landed and wrecked on its left side, blocking any access to the hold. Although Chisum

Before the 1983 accident, John Stimson checks crab pots aboard the P/V *Enforcer*.

pilots all carried a "ditty bag" with emergency items and a .357 sidearm, even that was compressed. Since Wiltrout was, for the most part, out of commission with a broken back, he was unable to help pry a way in. Though he tried, the bitter wind raking at him, Stimson could not break through to the survival gear by himself. There they remained—stranded, hurt, freezing—while inches away behind buckled metal lay warmth, food, and safety.

Through the long night, however, the downed survivors were not totally alone; above in the storm, two Elmendorf HC-130 communications aircraft alternated flights to keep the radio tuned to the ELT signal. They circled the area during the dark hours.

As best they could, Stimson and Wiltrout burrowed together trying to stay warm. Wiltrout's numb legs told him his feet were freezing. Sometime during the night, Stimson—either confused by hypothermia or in a last-ditch effort to find help—wandered away from Wiltrout. The next morning, the pilot managed to find him nearby, but the cold had taken his life.

By 6:00 the next morning, a Coast Guard H-3 helicopter arrived in Cordova. The chopper swung off immediately for the crash sites, but whiteout conditions pressed it back. The fierce winds picked up power as the morning advanced. Air Force weather reports noted "icing from the ground to 8,000 feet, visibility is 1/16 of a mile and winds are 35 knots, later gusting to 70 knots." Regardless, the H-3 finally spotted Ranney's position and tried to put down several times. Again, winds and whiteout made landing impossible. Rescue units simply could not risk another disaster. Through radio contact, however, Ranney assured them—she was cold, but OK.

At about noon the Coast Guard rescue helicopter made a visual sighting of Wiltrout's downed helicopter. With a reading on the position, the Coast Guard flew back to Cordova and prepared for rescue. At 2:30, the chopper returned, loaded with rescue workers and hypothermia expert Dr. Martin Nemiroff. At the crash site, the chopper hovered and started down. Then, just twenty feet from the ground, the nose of the helicopter jerked up. The pilot instantly compensated and regained control, but he sensed the hydraulic system had failed. The chopper malfunction left no choice but to return to Cordova with the rescue incomplete.

Below, Wiltrout's rising hope plummeted as he saw the chopper suddenly jerk up, change direction, and move away, the helicopter's motor fading into the storm. Daylight was fading, too, and Wiltrout knew he could not survive another night.

Fortunately the harsh weather broke, and a half-hour window of hope eventually opened. Winds and snows began to diminish—not much, but enough for another try. This time a state trooper aircraft—a Jet Master five-place helicopter—sent from Anchorage and piloted by Robert Larson, took advantage of the weather break. Without wasting time, he enlisted another trooper, Dan Decker, and the two lifted off from Cordova with one-half hour of daylight left. They took no more men in the chopper to leave room for the survivors if they made the rescue. It had to be then or never.

Sure of the location now and directed by the Elmendorf HC-130 above, Larson swung his chopper to the crash site in a final race with daylight. Zeroing in, the helicopter carefully hovered over the wrecked Ranger. Down, down it lowered, buffeted by the wind, visibility poor. Larson finally touched ground safely. There they found Stimson dead and Wiltrout in poor

Alaska State Trooper Bob Larson had a half-hour of daylight left to make the search.

condition.

The troopers quickly loaded and settled Wiltrout in the helicopter. Worried about darkness and the weather worsening, they sped next to Ranney's location and picked her up, barely crowding her into the chopper. With luck on their side this flight, the survivors arrived back in Cordova by 4:00 in the afternoon.

Doctors at the local hospital checked Ranney and released her. At the same time, rescuers placed Wiltrout on the Elmendorf HC-130 and flew him to an Anchorage hospital. On Saturday Larson returned to the Copper River area on a sad errand—to pick up the body of John Stimson.

Pilot Gary Wiltrout survived his ordeal. In Anchorage doctors used a new medical procedure that saved his feet from amputation. His back healed, but continued to cause pain occasionally. Presently he lives in Idaho with his wife and flies for a private logging company.

For his compassionate and unselfish actions to help save Ranney's and Wiltrout's lives, John Stimson was posthumously given the State of Alaska Award for Bravery-Heroism. Governor Bill Sheffield presented the medal to

Trish Stimson in February 1983 at ceremonies in Anchorage.

At the time of his death in 1983, John Stimson had a young son. Now grown, he lives in Cordova with a family of his own—a daughter and a son. The little boy is called John David Stimson after his grandfather.

Robert Larson received his State of Alaska Award for Bravery-Heroism at the same ceremony in February of 1983. The governor commended Larson: "In rescuing Gary Wiltrout and Gayle Ranney from their respective aircraft, you demonstrated great courage, valor, and skill. Without your actions, both well might have perished in that storm."

Larson lost his own life when a Bell 206 Long Ranger helicopter he was piloting crashed into Cook Inlet during a snowstorm in November 2001. Recently retired after twenty-one years as a civilian search-and-rescue pilot with the Alaska State Troopers, Larson, sixty, was flying for Era Aviation out of Anchorage. He had retrieved several FAA workers from a maintenance job on Fire Island. Two passengers survived the crash, but Larson and two others died.

On Larson's death, longtime friend and retired trooper Paul Burke said: "Besides his compassion for people, Larson flew a helicopter like no other. I think his DNA had gears and oil in it. When he went to a helicopter, he didn't so much fly it as wear it." ★

Governor William Egan pins the State of Alaska Award for Bravery-Heroism on Nancy Davis, Wien Airlines stewardess during the skyjacking in October of 1971.

# 2

# PUBLIC SAFETY RESCUES

Sometimes heroes are the people we hire to stand in harm's way, such as Alaska State Trooper Rose Edgren—who faced down a desperate and violent father in a domestic violence confrontation. But sometimes that hero is simply an employee of a private company serving the public. That was the case for young airline attendant Nancy Davis, who confronted a plane hijacker. In this section, you'll find two dramatic accounts of heroism in service to the public.

★

# SKYJACKED!

In a Boeing 737 over Alaska
and the Northwest, 1971

The Wien Airlines Boeing 737 Twinjet gained altitude out of Anchorage as it headed west on an early Monday morning flight toward Bethel, Alaska. The short days of October had arrived, and the aircraft labored up through dark skies. Thirty-one passengers settled in for the routine, hour-long trip.

Flight attendant Nancy Davis, twenty-two, might have been a little nervous that morning. This Bethel leg marked her very first time as a full-fledged stewardess, and she was determined to do a perfect job.

While she was setting up drinks in the galley, a thin young man with a moustache and small goatee looked in, asking her for the washroom. When he emerged, the next thing Davis knew, the deadly end of a .25-caliber automatic pistol pointed in her face. "We're not going to Bethel," he said. "I'm hijacking the plane. I want in the cockpit."

After a moment of stunned silence, Davis took a breath and kept her cool. Over the intercom to the cockpit, she alerted the crew through a coded system. Initially, thinking the new employee had made a mistake, Captain Don Peterson, forty-three, did not respond. When Davis repeated the code, he took her seriously.

At first, Peterson would not allow the cockpit opened. But the skyjacker grew more agitated and banged on the door. "He was really getting upset," Davis said, "waving the gun around and threatening to shoot out through the windows."

Finally the hijacker said to Davis, "Tell the captain he's got three minutes [to open the door] or I'm going to start firing." He said he didn't care what happened; he had nothing to lose.

To avert disaster, Peterson finally opened the cockpit door. There the hijacker voiced his demand: They were to fly south, maybe to another country. When the captain explained the fuel requirements for such a trip, the hijacker agreed to return to Anchorage.

First Officer Ray Miller radioed in the news: "I informed center that we were in the process of being hijacked." They called for confirmation from

Peterson, the pilot, and got it. "The center did not make any exclamation about it; they just approved our change of course," Miller said.

Meanwhile, the other flight attendant in the passenger section, Margie Hertz, located the hijacker's jacket in an overhead bin and found his parole card. He was Delbert Thomas, twenty-eight, a convicted felon.

Thus began the first skyjacking in Alaska history.

The Wien crew at first had no clue to Thomas's past. As evidence later revealed, he'd been tried in the first murder trial ever held in Kodiak—for the shooting of Kenneth Cherry in December 1965. Ultimately convicted of manslaughter, Thomas spent time in prison and finally returned to a Palmer correctional camp, where he was paroled in 1971, about two months before the hijacking. He told friends he was heading for Anchorage to look for work—his reason for leaving Palmer that week.

Earlier in the morning, before flight time, Thomas quietly tried to buy a ticket for an Alaska Airlines run. When he seemed unsure about his destination—Fairbanks or Seattle—the counter attendant put him off and notified airport security. Police checked only his green backpack and found no gun. According to airline officials at that time, a person could not be searched unless a detector signaled a dangerous object. Had Thomas continued into the Alaska Airlines waiting room, the gun would have been discovered by a metal detector. In 1971, Wien did not have this security equipment.

The hijacked Boeing returning to Anchorage touched down on the north-south runway normally used for small planes. Captain Peterson told Thomas the plane would be lighter and thus fly farther without people on board. Because of this, and Davis's persuasions, Thomas allowed the thirty passengers and one flight attendant to disembark while the plane refueled.

Outside, a refueling truck and a bus stopped near the cockpit so the hijacker could observe what was going on. While passengers deplaned, an FBI agent, unseen, lay flat on the bus floor ready to spring into action. The maneuver proved hopeless, however; he could do nothing without endangering other people. Peterson, copilot Ray Miller, engineer Keith Forsgren, and Nancy Davis remained on board.

Airline officials worried that Thomas would insist on flying west. During that era in history, bristly relations existed between the United States and Russia. If Thomas selected west as his choice, prompt arrangements had to be made to protect the Wien flight from being blown out of the sky on entering Russian air space. Plus, Don Peterson carried no Russian charts or maps on board. However, Thomas named Cuba as his destination, via Vancouver and then Mexico City for refueling.

Fourteen years after the skyjacking, Captain Don Peterson flies the first revenue flight of the new Wien Airlines, taking off in Anchorage.

Airline authorities asked Peterson to stall takeoff for twenty minutes. Unknown to the hijacker, officials alerted Elmendorf Air Force Base nearby. At 6:56 A.M., two F-4 Phantom jet fighters shot into the sky; orders called for them to shadow the Wien jet to the U.S. border. Canadian fighters would take over from there.

Authorities warned Kodiak, too. Within minutes, a Coast Guard C-130 lifted from the runway and pointed south in case the jet headed for Hawaii and had to ditch in the ocean should fuel run out.

The Wien crew, anxious and concerned, realized their unusual hostage position when the twinjet left the Anchorage runway. Once in the sky, few rescue options remained. No SWAT team or helicopter could swoop in and provide deliverance. And certainly Nancy Davis could not just flee out a door in an unguarded moment and obtain help. The crew was not in a position to act impulsively, to take a chance on overpowering Thomas, when one wrong move could speed them to crisis. Not while he held that gun in his grip.

The situation called for cool courage, sustained over hours, perhaps days. The crew had to move slowly, talk carefully. No one knew what tiny mistake or sudden action might trigger violence, plunging them all to certain death. And who knew what plight the crew faced when the journey ended, once the hijacker found safe haven—if they made it.

On the flight into Canada, Thomas settled with Davis in the cabin directly behind the cockpit, the gun always in evidence. Thomas asked for liquor, but

Davis said she didn't have the key to those supplies and served him coffee instead. She sensed he was coming off a high of some kind and was thinking more rationally as time passed by.

The skyjacker wanted to go to Cuba, and she tried talking him out of that destination. Davis told him if he went to Cuba he would probably spend some time in jail. "And the jails are awful in a Third World country. The language is different, and it's hot, and the food could give you dysentery." If he decided to give up, she persuaded, Canada or the United States would be better places. Davis presented a calm exterior, while in reality her "stomach was upside down."

During these conversations she learned the skyjacker had a history of problems. Recently paroled after conviction for the barroom killing in Kodiak, he had previously served time at McNeil Island Penitentiary in Washington State. Thomas revealed a particular aversion to going back to jail. He grew nervous and fidgeted when the topic came up, and Davis backed off the subject.

In spite of the danger, Davis felt sorry for the hijacker. He seemed depressed and down on life, she said. She thought him a mixed-up person, unstable certainly, but she could not hate him. "We talked about his different philosophies. . . . At one point he asked me what I was thinking about. I told him I was praying for him. He said no one had ever done that for him before."

Over the course of time, a vague brother/sister relationship developed. Davis's compassionate attitude helped defuse the tense situation. Captain Peterson's focus, however, was always on the weapon. "He had the gun in his hand about 90 percent of the time," the pilot recalled.

As Thomas and crew members talked in the cabin, Thomas often held the automatic in his grip. No one knew what word, or action, might set off the hijacker. Even during calm moments, Thomas played with the pistol or waved it around as part of his hand gestures when he spoke. Besides the weapon's immediate danger to life, the crew feared an accidental discharge. The twinjet was pressurized above eight thousand feet. At a cruising altitude of thirty-three thousand feet, quite a pressure differential existed between inside and outside the aircraft. A bullet shot through the window, shattering the outside pane, would cause an explosive decompression.

Peterson knew these risks. Before leaving the cockpit to talk to Thomas in the cabin, he ordered the copilot and engineer to don their oxygen masks. Then he told them: "If we have a problem, lose altitude as fast as possible. Get down low."

This potential calamity worried everyone as they flew on to Vancouver. The crew first learned of media attention focused on them while they cruised over Juneau. Peterson switched to a local radio frequency and heard commentator Al Bramstead speak of the hijacked plane, even as it flew overhead.

The jet eventually touched down on a rainy Vancouver runway about 11:00 A.M. to refuel. Pilot Peterson said he observed an overabundance of airport repair trucks, rollers, and road graders along the runway parking area. Unseen, behind each, Royal Canadian Mounted Police (RCMP) zeroed their rifles on the hijacked plane. The RCMP offered to come aboard and talk with the hijacker, but Thomas refused, warning them to stay 150 feet back from the aircraft. He would allow only a Western Airlines service employee on board, to bring in supplies and food.

With a gun leveled at her back, Davis lowered the rear stairs, and the "food attendant" boarded. Almost at once, she noticed the trousers of his service uniform—the leg hems had been cuffed up inside and stapled in place. Fortunately Thomas did not catch the deception. The RCMP "attendant" whispered for Davis to dash down the stairs and out of sight under the wing, but she declined, opting to stay with the crew. Nothing else could be done then, and the police "attendant" left the aircraft.

Forty-five minutes later, the Boeing lifted off for a four-and-a-half-hour flight to Mexico City. Don Peterson knew they would be cutting it close with fuel. Luck and winds with them, they could make Mexico City with only fifteen minutes of fuel to spare. But without the weight of passengers, the plane proved nose-heavy, and in that condition the jet needed added power and used more fuel.

As quiet and meek as Thomas appeared, the captain knew different. They were all sitting with a time bomb in their midst, and no apparent escape. Who knew the unstable nature of the man or what innocent remark might send him into a fury?

Nevertheless, as the flight headed south, Davis and other crew members spoke calmly with Thomas, discouraging him from his skyjacking plan while he paced up and down the aisle. "I'm just not sure Cuba is such a good idea," Thomas said, thinking out loud. In the end, the conversations swayed him. Flying somewhere over Salt Lake City, Thomas changed his mind. He decided to return to Canada and surrender to the RCMP.

About 12:45 P.M., Peterson radioed Vancouver to request the return. Officials told him to fly a wide bank in the turnaround, for above the aircraft, two fighters from McCord Air Force Base tracked their every move. The jets navigated in the blind spot above, so they could not be spotted from the aircraft.

Close to 2:00 P.M., the Wien flight landed again on the Vancouver runway. In the blazing lights from the parked plane, RCMP Inspector Bruce Northorp left his car in civilian clothes, opened his coat wide to show he was unarmed, and stepped up into the jet. A trained hostage negotiator, Northorp kept a low profile.

This Boeing 737 Twinjet is similar to the skyjacked Wien plane, with a range up to 2,500 miles.

It was a dire situation. Thomas, clearly tired but reluctant to give up control, waved the gun carelessly. When Davis told him to stop, Northorp blinked in surprise, not realizing the sibling-style relationship that had developed between the two. After a time, with Peterson's urging, Thomas allowed the engineer and copilot off the plane to eat. For an additional twenty minutes, Davis and Peterson sat with Thomas and Northorp, and talked.

Eventually, Northorp guaranteed Thomas a cell by himself during the night, but made no further promises. At last Thomas agreed to surrender. He would not, however, give up the gun until he left the aircraft.

About 3:00 P.M., Thomas permitted Davis and Peterson to leave Flight 15, so they stepped off the plane and onto the runway. But another thirty minutes of talk between Northorp and the hijacker passed before the two walked down the steps and onto the tarmac. There Thomas surrendered his gun, ending the ten-hour ordeal.

To avoid a mass of news media, the crew trailed RCMP officials to a small room for questioning. On the way through the crowd, Davis caught her name: "Nancy, Nancy!" It was her father, Charles Davis, a pilot for Western, who had heard of the hijacking in Seattle and followed his daughter to Vancouver.

Other Wien pilots flew the hijacked crew back north. After a series of stops, the crew landed in Anchorage the next morning.

The harrowing experience behind her, first-time flight attendant Nancy Davis still held her sense of humor. "I must say," she said, "I'm waiting to see what the second flight is going to be like."

Del Thomas did sleep in his own cell the first night in Canada. The next day authorities unceremoniously transported him to Blaine, Washington, and handed him over to the U.S. Marshal's office and the FBI. Officials then flew him back to Anchorage to answer air piracy charges. Concluding the court hearing, a judge added twenty years' confinement for hijacking to Thomas's parole violation.

Don Davis, head of the Palmer correctional camp from which Del Thomas was paroled before the hijack, could not believe Thomas would do such a thing. "He was always nice, shy, and a little withdrawn, but very friendly. Even as an inmate he was a good man to have around. We couldn't find enough work to satisfy his working need."

Palmer patrolman Bob Boyd had talked with Thomas the night before he left for Anchorage and the hijacking. At that time, Thomas confided to Boyd that he was thought to have committed a small robbery at his place of work, and he was innocent. He was worried about his parole. This burglary incident, plus his fear of returning to jail, might have prompted the hijacking the next day. In any case, anxious to escape, Thomas drove to Anchorage on Sunday, sold his car, and purchased a gun and airline ticket with the proceeds.

In December of 1971, Governor William Egan presented Nancy Davis with the State of Alaska Award for Bravery-Heroism for her major part in the peaceful conclusion of this skyjacking.

Other awards were also forthcoming. Peterson and Davis received the highest granted by the FAA—the Distinguished Service Medal. Both also attended the "Montreal Accords," sponsored by the United Nations, in an effort to deny refuge to hijackers in any country.

For a number of years after, Don Peterson flew for Wien, then Alaska Airlines, before retiring in 1988. Now he participates in Seattle aviation programs for the retired, enjoys his family, and travels.

But for Davis herself, the hijacking experience brought a beginning. At the time, Cliff Hollenbeck directed advertising and public relations for Wien, and he and Davis fell in love, marrying in Anchorage in 1972. After a short stay in the Orient, the couple moved to Ottawa, Canada. There they helped set up security for Canadian airlines.

As the year 1975 ended, the couple decided to work on their own and moved to Seattle, where they established a travel photography business they follow today. The Hollenbecks tour extensively while they write, direct, and film their projects, along with the ever-present leisure trips both enjoy. Nancy Davis has never really left airline travel; now, though, she flies as passenger instead of employee.

Looking back over the harrowing experience, Nancy Davis concluded that certain elements in her personal life helped bring about a satisfactory end to the skyjacking. First, her father piloted planes, and aviation terms, safety, and procedures were familiar to her. Next, because of her Alaska wilderness background, she had a vague acquaintance with guns; in fact, at one point in the flight, she insisted Thomas show her that the gun actually held bullets—she did not want to find out later that she had been held hostage with an unloaded weapon. Also, since Thomas appeared to be coming off a high of alcohol or drugs, Davis felt she was dealing with a child "out of control," where earlier teaching experience gave her support. And finally, her own youthfulness brought a nonthreatening element to the ordeal.

How did the experience affect her? "In public I'm more aware now," she said. "I'm not paranoid, but I focus on who is around me, what they are doing, and what I have to deal with in my surroundings. I'm just more aware." ★

★

# THE QUICK OR THE DEAD

## Delta Junction, 1995

Working as a state trooper in a small Alaska community has its drawbacks. A police officer may have only one officer backup, or none at all, when an emergency call flashes to the local unit. Alaska Trooper Rose Edgren of Delta Junction faced just such an emergency—along with a high-powered .30-06 rifle—one frigid day in February 1995.

Superiors and fellow officers thought highly of Trooper Edgren. So much so that, in 1993, "D" Detachment of the Alaska Department of Public Safety nominated her for the International Association of Chiefs of Police competition as "Outstanding Trooper of the Year." Later she finished as a runner-up in the national contest. But she was not just an outstanding police officer; she had an air of compassion that allowed her to understand both sides of a criminal complaint.

Delta Junction, where Edgren worked, was a town of about four thousand people at the time, kept alive by the construction of Fort Greely nearby and activities of the Alyeska Pipeline. The town expanded at the convergence of the Alaska and Richardson Highways, with vehicle traffic flowing through on the way in and out of Interior Alaska. Officers in this small town answered all initial local complaints—everything from vandalism to murder. The closest trooper support was in Fairbanks, one hundred miles away.

Because Delta Junction residents lived in a small town, authorities knew, for the most part, what went on, and who caused trouble. Forty-two-year-old Johnny K. Carter Sr. gained a questionable reputation around Delta Junction. Trooper Edgren had two prior police contacts with him.

On one occasion the winter before, Edgren answered an overdue (missing) report on Johnny Carter. She found him extremely intoxicated, wandering around in the Shaw Creek Flats area near Delta with temperatures in the minus-forty range. Because of Carter's drunken and frozen condition, Trooper Edgren had no trouble collaring and transporting him to Delta Junction.

On the second occasion, Trooper Edgren arrested Carter on a drunk-driving charge in November 1994. A check with the trooper's Fairbanks computer alert at the time revealed Carter had been involved in a domestic violence situation the year before and he could be "aggressively hostile" toward a trooper.

Alaska State Trooper Rose Edgren in 1995.

Many police officers will state that answering a domestic dispute call can be extremely dangerous. One Fairbanks officer remarked, "It's so volatile. People's emotions are running so high." Drinking can add explosive, irrational elements. An at-risk family often survived in an intense, terrorizing atmosphere.

Members of the Carter family lived this frightful existence, as evidenced by an earlier incident the very day Trooper Edgren faced her emergency outside town. As it turned out, her husband, Al Edgren, who worked for the Forest Service, literally uncovered the fear in the Carter household.

Al Edgren's first duty that early morning consisted of snowplowing the driveway leading to the Forest Service offices. Temperature: minus twenty-five degrees. As Al Edgren plowed, he noticed a "flash of pink in the ditch on the side of the road." Could that be a snowsuit, he wondered? Checking it out, he stooped at the gully and found a shaking, freezing eight-year-old girl lying there. Upon questioning, the girl identified herself as a member of the Carter family. She had missed the school bus, she stammered out, and was afraid to go home. Her father had been drinking and would beat her for missing the bus. Instead of returning home, she simply lay down, hiding in the snowy ditch. Al Edgren drove the girl to school and handed her to the principal for care.

Later that same day, Trooper Edgren faced her job with consequences that spelled life and death. Temperatures at the time passed minus thirty-five degrees, and kept dropping.

A 911 domestic disturbance phone call came in to the trooper office's dispatcher about 6:00 P.M. from the Carter home in a rural area outside Delta Junction. A woman, crying and upset, reported her boyfriend had been drinking, they had argued, and his mood had turned abusive toward her and the children. Since then he had stormed out of the apartment, and she thought he might have turned into the garage for more alcohol. The police dispatcher asked if weapons were involved, and the woman replied, "Not yet."

Troopers Edgren and Steve Bear answered the call, both of them "it," as there was no other backup. They had to handle the situation alone. Carter and his family lived in an apartment above a garage, with a stairway running up the left side to a personal entrance. Adjacent but detached was the home of Carter's in-laws.

When the troopers arrived, Edgren hurried up the stairs and talked with the woman at the door of her apartment while Bear remained below. The woman said Johnny was "rough with the children" and that he "pushed her against the wall, then slapped her along the side of her head." She thought he might be in the garage now. Trooper Edgren joined Bear at the foot of the steps, noticing the garage door open and the darkness inside. Could Carter be hiding there?

Trooper Bear had his back to the adjacent house, and as Edgren turned, she caught movement inside of a man's silhouette framed in the bay window. His shadow clearly signified to Edgren that the man carried a rifle in his hand. With both herself and Trooper Bear totally exposed, in the line of fire, Edgren could only react.

"He's got a gun!" she shouted to Bear, and pushed him to safety. They took cover at the side of the house.

Secure for the moment, Edgren heard the house door open and watched as the suspect stepped onto the porch, rifle at the ready. Thoughts of the children's safety in the apartment upstairs flashed through Edgren's mind. She called to the man twice, "Johnny, put down the gun," and ordered him to surrender, while Trooper Bear made his way around the back of the house trying to maneuver behind the suspect. As the seconds clicked by, Edgren drew her .40-caliber semiautomatic service revolver and stepped into view, facing Carter. Although it was dark, she could see him bringing down the deadly barrel of a .30-06, leveling it at her.

That moment turned into a "kill or be killed" situation.

As the suspect drew a bead on Edgren and shot, she fired one round from her pistol—nearly simultaneously. A deadly "bang, bang" shattered the air. Edgren's bullet ripped through Carter's left side, tore through his ribs, angled up, and lodged on the other side of his spine. Crying out, he crumpled onto the porch. Carter's bullet zipped past Edgren's hair and smacked into the garage, mere inches from her head. Edgren later said, "I'm convinced, if I hadn't fired, I wouldn't be here today."

Edgren's shot disabled Carter, and she and Bear began lifesaving procedures. Knowing Carter, and feeling sorry for him, Edgren kept asking, "Why did you make me shoot you?" He mumbled rather disjointedly about taking his nine-year-old girl, catching a plane the next day; he seemed depressed. Plainly, he thought he was dying.

Finally an ambulance arrived and rushed Carter to Delta Junction. From there a military helicopter flew the injured man to Fairbanks Memorial Hospital where doctors pronounced him in critical condition and held the prisoner under guard.

In Delta Junction that evening, a follow-up investigator checked the rifle Carter had used and found live rounds in the magazine, and one spent cartridge. The nearby wall, where Edgren had stood, revealed powder marks and a hole, supporting the trooper's statement.

A follow-up investigation of the in-laws' house revealed open red plastic ammunition boxes and other items strewn about the living room. Normally, the owner kept his guns unloaded in the bedroom and the ammunition separate in a spare bedroom. Carter had, undoubtedly, put the shells and rifle together for the deadly showdown. The in-laws were not home at the time.

Carter survived the incident and authorities detained him without bail at the Fairbanks Correctional Center. A week later a Fairbanks grand jury indicted him.

During the trial, Edgren surprised prosecutors by giving Carter a supportive hug before proceedings began. Yet on the witness stand, she displayed no emotion, but spoke decisively and professionally. In defense, Carter's attorney contended the accused was only bending forward to put the rifle down when he was shot. After deliberation, the jury returned with a guilty verdict of attempted murder. Judge Ralph Beistline sentenced Carter to eight years in jail.

In January 1996 Governor Tony Knowles presented the State of Alaska Award for Bravery-Heroism to Trooper Edgren in Juneau. "In the face of danger," the governor remarked of Edgren, "your heroic actions saved the life of your partner, yourself, and even your assailant."

As is normal procedure for troopers, Rose Edgren consulted with a psychologist after the shooting, though she experienced no particular anxiety or nightmares. Occasionally, however, her thoughts run through the deadly encounter. She sympathized with the Carter children in the apartment upstairs, and she felt relieved that Carter had lived. In the end, she said, "When I walked away, I knew I had done what I had to do. I knew there was no other way I could have handled it." ★

Searching for the lost hunters in the sea ice
off Saint Lawrence Island, June 1988.

# 3

# WATER AND FIRE RESCUES

With Alaska's vast coastline and inland rivers and lakes, it's no surprise that many rescues retrieve victims from waterways and seas. This is the largest collection of heroic tales in the book. Read dramatic, full-blown accounts of six Yup'ik hunters and a schoolteacher stranded on icebergs in the northern Bering Sea, of a toddler who slipped into spring-swollen Ketchikan Creek, or about the final voyage of the *Dora H.*, a fifty-three-foot fishing boat loaded with thirty thousand pounds of halibut.

Fire rescues have their own brand of terror. For investigators in the wake of a blaze, finding cause can be a dramatic detective story. In this section, read of the heroic but sad death of a young boy who collapsed while trying to save a family friend from a devastating fire in a small house where a friend and relatives slept one cold September night. Later investigators learned the fire was caused by arson. Who, how, and why were major questions they finally resolved. The answers only served to cast young Darin Olanna in the role of selfless hero.

★

# ADRIFT TO NOWHERE

## Off Saint Lawrence Island, 1988

At the beginning of June 1988, H. Vernon Slwooko Jr. (called Junior) of Gambell, Alaska, gazed out on the Bering Sea as crews readied about thirty-five boats for a hunt. Flocks of eider and old-squaw ducks flew over the water, tempting the hunter.

It was 7:00 in the evening, but no worry. Summer brought the light, all day and most of the night. In any case, hunts were not launched by clocks, but by men well experienced with the sea. They would be back in a matter of hours, hopefully loaded with ducks or anything else in their line of fire.

Shortly, two aluminum skiffs slid into the water. In the Slwooko party, Junior, thirty-nine, captained his boat with his two sons, Joe, eighteen, and Quinn, thirteen, and a cousin, Harold Slwooko, twenty-seven. A second boat carried more relatives and a friend: Mike Slwooko, thirty; Joe Slwooko Jr., thirty-five; and a thirty-year-old schoolteacher from Maine, Andy Haviland, who tagged along to snap wildlife photographs. The boats soon shoved off and motored away from land.

The northern section of the Bering Sea freezes during the dark months. As kinder weather arrives in spring, the ice breaks into giant slabs or icebergs. These clog the sea, drifted by the current and tossed by the waves until eventually they are carved away by warmer water. As the bergs move, water currents and countercurrent whirlpools determine their course. The bergs offer temporary ice platforms for animals and people. Formed mostly of snow, they also provide necessary fresh drinking water—before they melt away.

As Junior kept an eye on the sea, a message over his CB radio told of walrus to the northeast. The skiff headed there with the other boats, out of sight of Saint Lawrence Island. In a matter of hours, the hunters killed twelve walrus with their guns—nine for Junior's skiff. The men packed away the livers, hearts, special skin of the back, and the ivory tusks.

Soon, however, drifting ice began closing up again, forcing them to steer long channels around the floes, using up gas. Running short of fuel, they pulled up on a giant ice floe for the night, knowing friends from the island would motor out the following day with gas enough to bring them in. An evening fog rolled over the party as they settled down to sleep.

Junior Slwooko and the two boat crews near the coast of Russia.

Although the skies cleared the next day, the crews spotted no boats or land. For some reason, Junior's radio received messages but would not transmit.

The two boats headed south, and when they ran out of gas the men rigged sails from their ponchos. After traveling for several hours, the hunters realized they had probably missed the island and were adrift in the huge vastness of the Bering Sea.

The word "adrift" might give the impression of calm, leisurely floating, yet the men were often lifted on fifteen- to twenty-foot waves, ever working to hold the boats in the right position to keep from rolling over. Seven men, two open skiffs, limited food and water, a near-useless radio—they seemed to be rolling on an endless sea.

Meanwhile at Gambell, friends and relatives worried about the two skiffs when the hunters did not return at the expected time. Alaska troopers, Bering Air, and a Coast Guard C-130 began scouting over the weekend, but heavy weather restricted their search.

Those early days proved only the beginning of an intensive manhunt. It is difficult to convey the size of the search area, which contains only a few small, isolated islands as landmarks. In total, the expanse of the Bering Sea in square miles is one and one-half times larger than the entire landmass of Alaska. Add

The men set up temporary camp on an ice floe.

wind and fog to the vastness, plus the constant movement, and finding two eighteen-foot skiffs was like spotting two bottle caps on the ocean.

While out on the water, the seven Gambell hunters spent the first days on an ice floe—about sixty feet wide—eating walrus heart for food. Even on the ice they managed to build a fire, breaking plywood from one of the skiffs and cooking in an ammunition can, using it like a pressure cooker. Later they burned plastic pipes kept in the boats for rolling a vessel on shore. Often they ate any meat they could, raw. Regardless of their ingenuity, they had not brought along sleeping bags, and, whether they rested on a floe or in their boats, the damp worked into their bones.

Spotting no landmarks disoriented the missing men, and they thought the ice floe had drifted close to the Soviet coast. Then, as they camped, the floe itself began breaking up. Rotting icebergs can be dangerous as they break apart or turn completely over. At one point, melted chunks of ice high above on the iceberg loosened and began crashing down on their small camp, signaling it was time to move. With sea swells up to twenty feet, the men lashed the two boats together for stability and took off.

In spite of their cleverness, conditions were worsening. Their boats were out of gas, the fresh water was nearly gone, and their sustaining walrus meat was now rotting. The radio proved more a torment than a help—never enough power to get through, but never completely dead, either.

While the hunters ate raw any ducks they could shoot, retrieving the birds proved tricky until logistics furnished the answer. The birds had to be shot close enough to the boat's bow so that as the skiff passed the fallen duck, a hunter could scoop it up. Nevertheless, birds were not enough, and each day the men grew weaker.

The hunters did what they could. A walrus hide between the aluminum boats kept the skiffs from working into each other and causing damage. Out came a wooden seat from one boat to fashion a needed rudder for the other. Utilizing ice poles for masts and ponchos for sails, they managed to give some direction to their crafts. "It was like the Vikings," one hunter said.

Occasionally potential rescue tantalized the survivors; several commercial air flights flew high overhead and a number of distant ships streamed by. At one point they heard a fog horn blast through the mist, but the ship never materialized. The men shot off flares, fired rifles, but their actions proved fruitless.

During the long, empty days, the men daydreamed and talked, trying to keep a positive view. But questions came to mind: Would they ever see their families again? Would they come out of this alive? Or would their bleached bones be found on a distant shore by some casual beachcomber? Each man knew his window on life was slowly closing.

Captain of the main boat, Junior Slwooko brought a steady, positive spirit to the drifting group. Most of all, he stopped arguments, any of which might have turned survival into disaster. The boring, hopeless days eroded the men's confidence. Their thirst for food and water weakened them and brought on hopelessness. At times they picked at each other, found fault, and spoke of dying. Junior would not allow it. "I always knew deep in myself that we would make it . . . ," he said.

Obtaining fresh water proved a serious problem. When they could, the men melted ice, but after that disappeared they rinsed their mouths with seawater. Constant exposure to salt water chapped their lips, and when the waves showered on them the spray burned their faces and eyes until they could hardly see.

Every day the effort to survive grew more difficult as starvation and dehydration carved away at their spirits and their bodies. The men could not know their tiny skiffs had floated south, out of the expected search area. Nor could they know that, after two weeks, many of the scouting units weren't even looking for them anymore.

That first week of the search, Saint Lawrence Islanders picked up a few weak radio transmissions from the missing men. They said they seemed in good health but could not orient themselves as to direction—heavy fog obscured any landmarks.

During that time, determined rescue crews converged on Saint Lawrence Island. Alaska State Troopers, the U.S. Coast Guard, civilian units, and the Army National Guard concentrated on the search, along with village residents. The Coast Guard cutter *Midgett* arrived offshore and took command as on-scene coordinator. A California-based anthropological research ship, the *Hawaiian Tropic Cyrano*, already in the area, soon added its support to these vessels.

Additionally, in spite of political differences between the United States and Russia, the Soviet Maritime Rescue Service offered help. The Russian government also allowed three Alaska National Guard UH-60 Twin Otters to fly reconnaissance over controlled foreign territory. The Otters' two flights over restricted water and shoreline were the first American visits since World War II.

Yet searchers found nothing.

Thinking it the most promising location, rescue crews focused on the area north and northeast of Gambell. Coast Guard and National Guard planes combed the expanse, along with the Civil Air Patrol. Dirty pack ice, northward currents, and the possibility of mistaking walrus for men complicated the search.

For days the search proceeded. The skies, filled with heavy fog, limited visibility. By the end of a week or so, the weather cleared. That in itself proved frustrating, for though it opened the vast ocean sweep to view, searchers still could not spot the hunters.

Villagers, however, kept confident, for the hunters had several pluses to their credit. Aside from being fairly young, all but one were seasoned seamen and hunters. They could read the weather and water. These skills had kept their ancestors alive for centuries. This knowledge did not guarantee safety, but it gave the hunters a needed edge.

On June 11—about ten days into the search—Savoonga hunters found footprints on a thirty-five-mile-long ice floe. Weather closed in, however, and forced the men to return to Saint Lawrence Island. When the skies opened again, Savoonga searchers knew it would be futile going back.

"With the currents, God knows where it [the floe] is now," National Guardsman Harry James stated. "And in the last few days, the bigger floes have really begun to break up."

The third week of the search, the Soviets pulled out. The Coast Guard suspended operations after scanning for fifteen days, spending a quarter of a million dollars and finding nothing.

"We exhausted every possibility," said Captain Michael Stenger, chief of Juneau Search and Rescue. "We searched, re-searched, and re-re-searched."

Two of the lost hunters—Harold and Michael—were members of the Alaska Army National Guard, and that organization, along with villagers, would not give up.

"The fact that we have not located any debris is good," reported Alaska National Guard Major General John Schaeffer. "It means that it is likely the boats are intact, upright, and the hunters are surviving somewhere on an ice floe from their hunting and fishing."

Though villagers remained alert, hope of finding the lost men alive faded. After all, the Gambell hunters had been out nearly twenty days with no clue to their whereabouts. They had left with one day's food supply but had killed walrus, so they would not starve—at least not right away. Townspeople counted on the men's ingenuity. Water would be the serious problem—the hunters required fresh water. Although villagers added up positives to keep their hopes up, the actual picture grew grimmer as the days and weeks passed. Where were they? Where could they be?

The Bering Sea, however, was not to claim these men. After nearly three weeks, luck and weather turned. The currents and the fickle wind finally changed and blessedly guided the boats north again.

When Junior, ever watchful over the sea, spotted mountaintops in the distance, it proved an exhilarating sight. He lifted his voice and shouted, "Land ahoy!" and everyone's spirits soared—a moment of pure joy.

On reflection, the hunters figured they might be near Siberia, then changed their minds. The days still held low fog, and visibility was poor. Or could they have drifted near Golovin Bay on Alaska's mainland east of Nome? Actually the hunters did not care where they were; land—any land—meant fresh water and food, and, as Junior said, ". . . we were rejoicing like hell."

Half a day of intense paddling went by as the men worked to position the boats close enough to shore. With a twelve-foot surf rolling in, beaching would be a problem. After all they'd been through, they couldn't risk a disaster—not at the very moment of victory.

For safety's sake, the hunters decided to land in a single boat. They loaded one skiff with all the gear; in the bottom, tied-down empty gas cans added flotation. Then Junior positioned paddlers with makeshift oars along the sides.

Junior Slwooko and his sons rejoiced at landing on Saint Lawrence Island
after their three-week ordeal.

At just the right moment, as someone dropped the sail, Junior yelled, "Paddle, paddle, paddle!" Using a last spurt of energy, the hunters dug in.

As the wave rose, the boat lifted, riding along on the crest until it washed on the beach, landing safely. The survivors—wet, blistered from seawater, and with swollen feet—stumbled ashore, grateful to feel the solidness of ground under them.

Once on the beach, Junior drew out his binoculars. Sighting over the terrain, he recognized Mountain Invut, and a cheer ran through him. They had landed not in Siberia or on the mainland, but right at home, on Saint Lawrence Island! Even in their run-down condition, the news elated them. Junior knew of a cabin about ten miles away, and, with no other option, they planned to try for that.

While Andy and Harold stayed and built a fire, Junior and the rest of the crew straggled off to find food, returning with fresh water, ducks, and eggs. After eating, Junior took the near-dead CB radio to a high spot in hopes of reaching people in Savoonga, some forty miles away.

On the research vessel *Cyrano*, however, Dennis James, a Gambell hunter himself, caught the weak signal coming from the south side of Saint Lawrence Island, not far from their position. At first he could not believe it. But it was true—a transmission sent by the missing hunters. Right then he notified Gambell and the National Guard.

By 7:30 P.M., the National Guard's Blackhawk helicopter from Nome swooped down through heavy fog closing in over the southeast cape of Saint Lawrence Island, trying to spot the landed survivors.

"A flare was shot off about a hundred yards directly in front of us as we came in for what would be the pickup," National Guard pilot Terry Cartee stated. "The fog was so thick it was hard to move."

Once down, guardsmen loaded the hunters into the chopper, thus ending the twenty-two-day ordeal at sea. Survival and rescue—an unbeatable combination.

Junior felt sure they could have made the cabin without the rescue helicopter. "But it would have been difficult," he said. "Mike, Andy, and Harold were walking around like robots."

And they might not have made it, too, as all the survivors needed medical attention. Three weeks of starvation, dehydration, and malnutrition might have claimed a life or two.

"They were in pretty bad shape," said Mike Haller of the Army National Guard. "It was the grace of God and angels they got back. Like a baseball game. They made third base, and the Blackhawk brought them home."

When word reached Gambell, happiness swept through the Slwooko family. "Oh boy, I got chills up and down my body, back and forth," said relative Holly Slwooko. "Everybody's going house to house, visiting, hugging and kissing. We're planning a big feast when everything calms down."

Gambell townspeople could hardly contain themselves to welcome the hunters, but low fog kept the helicopter from landing. Instead the chopper flew to Savoonga, where all five hundred residents gave the survivors a hero's welcome, swarming around the helicopter in an embrace before it had time to cut the engine. Even the dogs howled in welcome.

Four of the weary hunters stayed in Savoonga overnight. Guard members immediately medevacced the other three survivors to Anchorage on the Alaska Air Guard C-130 for medical attention. Despite the hunters' mild frostbite, dehydration, and malnutrition, Anchorage doctors pronounced them in fair shape, and they soon recovered.

A happy upshot of the ordeal was the marriage of Holly Slwooko and Andy Haviland on July 9, three weeks after the rescue. They had been going together for several years, but the sea experience helped Andy decide that life was too short.

Because of their courage and determination on this rescue, members of the Alaska Army National Guard received the State of Alaska Award for Bravery-Heroism. Governor Steve Cowper boarded a C-130 on August 15, landing at Gambell, Savoonga, and Nome to present the medals and other awards.

"People from around the state and around the world were watching," Cowper noted, "and the search was a success. There's lots of credit to be spread around here."

That three-week search proved a triumph for rescue units and the residents of Saint Lawrence Island—all the searchers who ventured into ominous weather to look for the men. The same could be said for the seven lost Saint Lawrence walrus hunters, who made those grueling weeks a challenge of survival.

Having been lost at sea has not stopped Junior Slwooko from hunting. But he checks weather and sea conditions more thoroughly now. And, he makes sure he has freshly charged batteries for his CB radio.

Did the ordeal change his life?

"I appreciate life more now," he said. "The little things. I respect each day for what it brings." ★

★

# NO OTHER CHOICE

## Scout Lake, 1968

Winter ice finally cleared from Scout Lake near Soldotna on a May Saturday in 1968—the water still bitterly cold, but calm. The Prinzing youngsters played outside all afternoon, enjoying the sunny weather despite a decided sharpness in the air. Everyone wore thick clothing and heavy rubber boots to ward off the chill. Suppertime was drawing near, but spring brought long days, and plenty of light filled the air. Time for a quick cruise on the lake.

Twenty-six-year-old ex-Marine John Paul Franklin launched his twenty-foot, inboard/outboard, fiberglass-and-wood boat down an incline into the water. Then he called the Prinzing kids—friends he knew who lived near the lake—and loaded them on: Ronnie, three; Randy, thirteen; Nancy, twelve; Ricky, eleven. John Paul also invited his twenty-year-old fiancé, Kathleen Robinson, along for the ride. The boat rode low in the water, but no wind stirred, and the lake held only a slight ripple.

Randy remembered that day, remembered shoving the boat into the water, remembered the boat drifting out.

About a hundred feet from shore, Franklin yanked the start rope on the motor. The Mercury inboard/outboard backfired and would not kick in. Lifting the cover, Franklin looked in and spotted a fire starting. He tried putting it out, but couldn't find the gas line cutoff. Some of the gas leaked onto the floor of the skiff, mixed with the water there, and flared up in no time. In moments flames roared to life and soon consumed the stern. The motor could explode any second.

By now smoke filled the air as the blaze spread. Everyone crowded to the bow, coughing, the flames scorching them. They'd have to swim for it. John Paul, a strong swimmer, slid over the side, and Randy handed his three-year-old brother down to the young man. Then the others jumped in and started making for shore.

No sooner had Randy and Nancy hit the surface than the shock of the icy water took their breath away. Randy could hardly speak and found himself puffing, sucking for air at every stroke. Together they struggled for land side by side, sinking, dragging themselves up. Nancy finally gasped out, "Can't . . . can't make it. . . ."

"You . . . have to," Randy managed, taking her hand. "Keep swimming." Stroking ahead, weighted by his soggy clothes, Randy pulled her along, swam ahead, and then drew her along again. The freezing water drained warmth from their bodies, leaving them numb and exhausted. Finally, convinced they could go no further, their feet at last touched something solid. Weak, shivering, gasping for air, they dragged themselves on land.

Collapsing with the safety of shore under him, Randy heard his brother, Ricky, out on the lake, calling for help. Ricky could only dog paddle. Randy did not think he could survive going out again. Next to him, injured with first-degree burns, Nancy urged him to go. Neither could disregard the call for help. There was no choice.

Chilled to the core, Randy stripped off his sodden woolen clothing, his shirt and pants, his boots, and dove back in. He focused on reaching his brother and bringing him to shore.

No sooner did Randy approach than his brother, in a panic, clutched him and climbed him like a tree. Ricky kicked and pushed to get on top of Randy, forcing him under the water. Every time Randy surfaced, Ricky grabbed him and mounted again. Randy gulped for air, wrestling with his brother, desperately trying to stay on top. At last, the older boy shook himself free, dove well under the water, and broke the surface a short distance from Rick. "You can't . . . do that!" he shouted, his teeth chattering. "Stop climbing—I can't swim."

The warning got through. The next time Randy swam over and offered his back, Ricky hung on, and Randy struggled with him to land.

When they arrived, Ricky slipped from Randy's back, both of them falling to the shore. Nancy, hurting from her burns but somewhat revived, told Randy Kathleen could not swim, only float. Gazing out, Randy spotted Kathleen still on the lake, far out, trying to stay on top of the water. A quick glance showed no sign of John Paul and Ronnie.

Exhausted and numb, hardly thinking, Randy dove in yet another time, swimming to Kathleen. She was floating, holding on to a piece of debris, still on her back. Randy gripped a hand and sidestroked toward the beach, gliding the floating Kathleen along. Weak and dazed, they eventually made shore, as she proved the easiest to bring in.

Randy's father, Reuben Prinzing, quickly learned of the emergency. "I was at the Sterling School getting my car washed and someone told me my children had drowned in Scout Lake. When I got to the lake, I found out from some

Scout Lake on the Kenai Peninsula.

friends that ... they were all in the boat and it caught fire. They all swam ashore except Franklin and little Ronnie."

Franklin and young Ronnie never made it. Private divers located their bodies hours after, about fifty feet from shore. Once overboard, experts surmised, the shock of icy water took Franklin down, and Ronnie too. The hospital report further explained: Franklin's lungs had been seared badly by the fire. Relatives held funerals for the two victims in the following days.

Never reported was the fact that the burning boat tragedy was the second incident that day in which thirteen-year-old Randy risked his life. On Scout Lake that morning, a seven-year-old fell from a homemade raft; Randy swam out, caught the youngster, and stroked with him to shore and safety.

Randy's unselfish bravery might have passed unnoticed except for a memo sent by Trooper Lawrence of the Kenai Detachment, which recommended the medal for the teenager. In the fall, the governor's office notified Randy of the

John Paul Franklin during his U.S. Marine days. Franklin drowned in Scout Lake while attempting to save young Ronnie Prinzing.

honor, and Governor Walter Hickel presented the award at the Soldotna Community Hall in October.

"The occasion which brings us together today is a sad one," Governor Hickel said in his ceremony speech, "sad because it was marked by a tragedy which took the lives of two persons. . . . But while this occasion is tinged with sadness, it is also a time for us to take a moment to point with pride to the achievements of another young man, and to pay him honor for the part he played in saving the lives of two others."

The total story did not end with the Scout Lake misfortune, for an echo of the tragedy touched John Paul Franklin's family twenty years later. When ex-marine Franklin died at Scout Lake in 1968, he left a three-year-old son, John Paul Jr., living at Clear, Alaska. In the mid-1980s, when this boy reached his early twenties, he was driving near a wilderness lake in Wisconsin; no guardrail ran along the road. The auto hit gravel, spun out of control, and John Paul Jr.'s car catapulted into the lake. The young man drowned, just like his father almost twenty years before.

The Prinzings did not remain in Alaska, but moved back to the family home in Minnesota. Nancy and Ricky both married and have jobs there, as do Randy and his wife, Judy. In August of 2000, the two boys and their parents returned to Alaska for a week, where they visited little Ronnie's grave.

The tragedy at Scout Lake haunted Randy emotionally for years. At first he considered himself a failure, because two people had died. Not until he matured into his twenties did he turn that blame around. Now he feels better about himself, knowing Ricky, Nancy, and Kathleen survived because of him. ★

★

# FIGHT FOR LIFE

Buckland, 1989

About forty miles south of the Arctic Circle and sixty-five miles southeast of Kotzebue clusters the small community of Buckland, along the Buckland River. Flooding in the flatlands has forced the residents to move, at times, from one site to another. Freshwater lakes dot the area; at one of these lakes on the weekend of October 15, 1989, several teenagers attempted a daring rescue.

Saturday morning, Evans Geary and three student friends—Johnny Sheldon, Jason Rutman, and Jessie Ahkpuk Jr.—wandered out to one of the small lakes outside Buckland. Cold chilled the air and the boys wore sweaters and jackets. Although it was already 11:00 in the morning, the winter sky only shortly before had opened toward daylight.

With the dark months approaching, the lakes had iced up since September and boys and girls skated on the surface. But crowding prevented everyone from using the smaller pond close by, and a group of youngsters made their way to a more spacious lake—one they called Two-Mile Lake. Evans and his friends, goofing around, wandered over to Two-Mile to check out the surface and see how safe it was. Some of the kids were already there.

Arriving, the older boys ran and slid onto the ice, while fifteen feet behind followed Fred Lee and Carl Hadley, both about eight years old, ice skating. Everyone was having a good time, laughing and calling while they spread out and slid along. As the young boys got closer to the middle, Jason shouted, "Hey, guys. Don't go too far."

The warning, however, sounded too late. Suddenly the surface gave an ominous "*crack!*" webbing outward. "Get off! Get off the ice!" the teenagers shouted.

The older boys heard Fred and Carl, a distance away, cry out in surprise, and Jason shouted, "Hey, look! They fell in." Both youngsters, three feet apart, had crashed through, opening a jagged hole about ten feet across, and disappeared under the freezing surface of the water.

In seconds, the teenage boys flattened on the ice, carefully sliding along and forming a human chain over the weak ice to the opening. Carl was closest, and with careful movements they managed to pull him out without breaking through themselves.

Fred Lee finally surfaced and thrashed about on top but could not stay up, the frigid water pulling strength from his body. Without thinking, Evans focused on the young victim, peeled off his outer clothing, and jumped in. No time to be afraid. Down he plunged, the icy lake water knifing his skin as it closed over his head—the shock taking his breath away. But he fought, struggled to the surface, located Fred a distance away, and swam across.

Diving under, feeling drained himself because of the cold, Evans grabbed the front of Fred's jacket. By now Fred had lost consciousness, and the body pushed through the water as a dead weight. Evans pulled Fred up and lifted his head above the surface. With Fred in his right hand, pushing ice away with his left arm, Evans swam as best he could.

When Evans reached the edge of the ice and tried to hand Fred up to the human chain, the waterlogged body proved too heavy. Under the added activity and weight, the ice cracked, and Jessie and Johnny fell into the frigid water too.

When they surfaced, the boys managed to drag and pull themselves—and Fred—off the ice and onto shore. Jason Rutman ran for help.

Fred Lee showed no vital signs of life. No breath, no pulse, and every muscle limp in death. While Johnny held Fred's head to keep the air passage open, Evans began mouth-to-mouth resuscitation, the two taking turns.

Urgently the boys worked over Fred—press . . . release . . . press . . . release . . . breathe—while the other boys hollered and screamed at Fred, trying to pierce his darkness and spark some reaction from his body. Evans and Johnny kept working, not giving up.

At long last, Fred gave a shudder, a cough, and began spitting up water. A sense of triumph and relief shot through the older boys. At the same time they knew Fred needed medical help and warmth to keep his heart going. Jessie picked up Fred in his arms and began stumbling toward the clinic in Buckland, a mile away.

By this time Jason neared town and ran to Del Thomas's house, rousting him out. Quickly, Jason explained what had happened and pointed to the group behind. Thomas jumped on his track vehicle, and even though there wasn't enough snow yet, he took off. Thinking the boys might need more assistance, Jason flagged down a lady on a four-wheeler and asked her to get help.

Thomas's machine could not travel over the thin ice of the lake, so it circled around to Jessie, who held Fred in his arms. Checking Fred's vital signs, Thomas found the young boy still breathing and loaded him on the snowmobile. From there they sped to the clinic, where Dr. Kennedy treated Fred for hypothermia.

Fred Lee, who nearly drowned in a Buckland lake in 1989, is alive and kicking, thanks to Evans Geary and his friends. Lee competed in the 1999 World Eskimo-Indian Olympics in Fairbanks.

For several hours Fred Lee remained at the clinic, with Kennedy examining his progress, keeping a close eye on body temperature and vital signs. Fred complained his chest hurt, but the doctor found it clear, and knew Fred would be all right. When everything checked out—Fred spelled his last name as a final mental test—the doctor released him.

Temperature in the clinic proving none too warm, Thomas carried the small boy to his house close by. There Thomas wrapped Fred in blankets and put him to bed, placing a bowl near in which to spit lake water if need be.

Meanwhile, news of the rescue passed through the village. Evans, drenched, chilled to the core, was just leaving the trail onto the road to town when his parents picked him up and took him home.

For their unselfish rescue of Fred Lee, Senator Al Adams recommended the heroism award for the four boys. Governor Steve Cowper presented the State of Alaska Award for Bravery-Heroism in the Buckland school gym that November.

"Teamwork is key to many challenges, and this emergency was no exception," the Governor stated. "Taking responsibility for others, especially when it means risking one's life, demonstrates great bravery."

In a press statement released by the governor's office, Chuck Greene, mayor of the Northwest Arctic Borough, said, ". . . the teenagers performed an exceptional act of bravery and courage. The experience of reviving a life is something some of us may never experience. All of us can be very proud of these young heroes."

Where did young people such as Evans and Johnny, in a remote community, learn CPR? NANA Corporation ran a five-week summer camp for youngsters in the area, called Sivunniigvik, a word in the Inupiaq language that means "a place where you plan." The camp offered specialized programs, depending on who was available to teach. Activities varied—everything from water safety to mapping to constructing fishing nets to rifle safety, and much more. Evans Geary took a class in CPR at the camp—and it saved Fred Lee's life.

An Alaska state trooper at the time, Roy Harper, now living in Wyoming, spoke to the determined attitude of the residents. He said, "People in the Northwest never give up. When troopers or rescue people know someone is alive, they give their all. When troopers know the person is dead and it's strictly body recovery, then finding them goes down on the priority list. But that is not so for the people up there. They go full out for a lost person whether they are alive or known dead. They never give up."

The boys never gave up on Fred Lee, either.

The young rescuers have grown and scattered since the accident—Jason is married, living in Anchorage, working near Kotzebue. Johnny lives in Kotzebue, while Jessie remains in Buckland. Evans Geary has moved around in a number of jobs. Several years ago Evans trained for employment at Red Dog Mine, and he presently works for that organization in Anchorage.

The rescued Fred Lee reported a fear of water for a time following his accident, but overcame that. The near-drowning experience did not permanently harm him physically as later activities demonstrated. After graduating high school, Fred participated in the World Eskimo-Indian Olympics at Fairbanks in July of 1999 where he competed in the Alaskan high kick event. As for an occupation to pursue, he hopes to obtain training in carpentry and work in Buckland.

About his near-death experience so many years ago, Fred had one piece of advice, which he says with a smile in his voice: "Don't walk on thin ice." ▣

# SPECIAL DELIVERY

### Ketchikan, 1965

Residents of Ketchikan, Alaska, were enjoying one of their clear August days in 1965. Many lingered outside to appreciate the day's sunshine. No one suspected an urgent crisis on such a peaceful Monday.

Albert Rothfuss, twenty-two, a deliveryman for the Ketchikan Soda Works, thought it a fine day for making his collection rounds. A Ketchikan resident for more than ten years, Rothfuss knew the town and its residents. He drove to liquor stores and grocery markets, noting his collections and stuffing coins and bills into his pockets. He pulled up near the harbor to finish some paperwork.

Emily Guthrie, two, was outside enjoying the sun. She romped with her brother and sister on a bridge straddling Ketchikan Creek near the middle of town. The bridge bordered a section of the Guthrie's front yard, and the children played there often.

"Creek" hardly described the swollen, deep, fast-flowing water below; "river" would have been more accurate. A plunging waterfall above the creek produced a roiling, folding current.

Emily's older sister, Sandy, kept an eye on the young children. She checked on them, then headed back inside. What caused her to glance back, she would never know. But when she did, Emily had disappeared.

After a dazed instant, Sandy's stomach tightened. She dashed to the handrail, guessing the only possible answer: Emily had fallen through a space between bridge and railing. Down below, little Emily struggled in the creek, clutching her hollow rubber doll. Air in the doll may have helped buoy her on the surface.

Sandy bolted around the bridge railing, screaming, slipping, stumbling down the bank. She tried stepping out into the creek, but the current boiled past, and Sandy couldn't swim. The snow-fed creek churned in the center, taking Emily along. Sandy watched in horror as the current pulled her little sister under, then bobbed her to the surface again, over and over like a crazy rubber ball.

Emily's mother heard the screams. Joined by others, she ran to the creek and along it, in a panic to reach her Emily. She feared her little girl had been

Al Rothfuss in Ketchikan (1967), just after receiving the heroism medal and just before leaving for a military tour in Vietnam.

in the creek too long; how could any baby live through that? The family had already experienced one tragedy; Emily's father had died two years earlier, while her mother was pregnant with Emily.

Ahead, Emily rolled along, face down now. If someone did not stop her before she reached the channel, she could be washed away into Thomas Basin, then Tongass Narrows, and possibly lost forever.

In a few short minutes, Emily drifted to the last bridge, where the creek widened out into the channel of Thomas Basin. The fire department arrived and several men raced to the boardwalk overpass, vaulted the railing, and tried reaching the girl. None of them made it.

In the federal building across the street from the creek, twenty-four-year-old Coast Guard Yeoman Mark Zartarian heard commotion through an open, second-story window. A father himself, Zartarian had five years in the service and had recently been transferred from Station Kodiak. Immediately he made for the stairs and headed for the harbor.

Rothfuss, standing close by his delivery truck, heard townspeople's frantic screams for help. Dropping his work, Rothfuss rushed to the channel, spotting a "blue something" that surfaced on the far side. Also a father, Rothfuss didn't hesitate; he launched himself into the freezing water. He disregarded danger to himself, forgetting the several pounds of change stuffed in his pockets. He was certain that if he didn't reach the child, she might not make it.

The minute Rothfuss hit the water, he lost sight of his target, but people onshore shouted directions as he swam. Emily's mother stood by, sending desperate prayers to the swimmer.

Cold, winded, fighting to grasp the child, Rothfuss finally reached her. He snagged Emily's hair close to the scalp, gripped it tightly, and thrust her head out of the water. But on that side of the channel, he confronted a twenty-foot

Ketchikan Creek runs swiftly through downtown Ketchikan
and empties into Tongass Narrows.

breakwater. He couldn't get her out that way. Weakened by the icy water, he began struggling back to the other side. Halfway to safety, he "started running out of gas"—unsure he could make it. Still he kept on, dragging his arms through the current in spite of the numbing cold and exhaustion. Finally spent, weighted down by the coins in his pockets, he went under. When his feet touched bottom, he walked toward shore under the surface, all the while holding Emily high above his head and keeping her face out of the water as much as possible.

At last, Rothfuss got close to the other side. Yeoman Mark Zartarian had slipped down the steep bank into the knee-deep water. He reached for Emily and lifted her out. With the help of many hands, Rothfuss dragged himself up the slope and collapsed on shore.

Emily showed no signs of life—no pulse, no breathing, her skin holding a deep blue cast. Zartarian began mouth-to-mouth resuscitation, repeating and repeating the cycle. Was the urgent rescue to no avail? Hope seemed to fade with each passing moment. Still, he did not give up.

After about eight minutes, the little body shuddered. Emily spit out water and began coughing and crying—the sounds sending triumph through the air. State Trooper Terry McConnaughey rolled a blanket around the tiny girl, handed her into a waiting patrol car, and raced with her to the Ketchikan General Hospital. The child was saved, police officer William Klein said, "just in time. Another minute and she would have been out into the channel."

Radio officer W. E. Greer Jr., from the SS *Arizona Standard* had witnessed the rescue and followed Rothfuss around the side of a building to thank him.

Interviewed later, Greer praised police and people's involvement. "I was mostly impressed by the young man who went courageously to the rescue, and the other who breathed life into the child. It was a perfect accomplishment, and I am proud to have seen it."

Zartarian, wet and sweaty, returned to his office in the federal building. Unaware of the rescue, his boss raised an eyebrow at the yeoman's soiled appearance, nodded rather crossly toward the counter, and said, "You've got a customer there." Only fifteen minutes later did the boss find out what had happened, when a state trooper entered the office and congratulated Zartarian. "Nice job," the officer said. "She's going to make it."

A letter from Alaska Coast Guard Commander George Synon followed, commending Zartarian for his ". . . alertness, quick thinking, and prompt and efficient manner . . ." in saving the child.

Emily Guthrie remained in the hospital for about a week while her lungs healed. Zartarian and Rothfuss visited her, bringing a teddy bear, and—Emily remembered—three packs of gum.

While in the hospital, Emily spoke of a strange occurrence. Although she had never seen her father alive, and photographs of him were rare, she told her family, "I saw Daddy." As she had returned to consciousness, her father had appeared in her mind, urging her on toward life, she said. Family members still speak of this experience.

A letter from Carl Mathisen of the Alaska Army National Guard in Ketchikan informed the governor of Rothfuss's heroic action. For his daring rescue at risk to his own life, Governor William Egan authorized the State of Alaska Award for Bravery-Heroism be conferred on Albert Fred Rothfuss. This was the first heroism award and the medal was not yet struck; the actual ceremony took place in Ketchikan in the fall of 1967.

Today Emily and her family live in Santa Fe. Zartarian, father of four, retired from the Coast Guard and works now as an emergency management director and full-time firefighter in New Hampshire. Rothfuss left Ketchikan, joined the Army, and served in Vietnam. Pipeline construction eventually brought him back to Alaska. Now retired, he lives in Copper Center with his second wife, Gretchen. ★

# THE VERY EDGE OF DEATH

Near Sitka, 1987

Commercial fisherman Jim Blades of Sitka, Alaska, and his son, Clinton, weren't looking for any trouble on December 10, 1987. The summer fishing season had been good, but catching a few additional winter kings would help pay Christmas bills, that's all. Clinton, a useful deckhand even at age six, always enjoyed going out with his dad. So, facing into a cold wind, with gray skies overhead, they left the Sitka harbor in their seaworthy twenty-six-foot wooden fishing troller, *Bluebird*.

Because the salmon continued biting, the pair fished all day on the open sea. The swells rolled in higher than normal, but these two fishermen had experienced that before. With Lady Luck riding their wake, both fishermen were reluctant to leave the fishing grounds and stayed out longer than intended.

By 4:00 P.M., darkness settled in. Since the weather broadcast warned of a small craft advisory, Blades decided to stay in the area rather than try for home. The skipper radioed his wife, Jill, who was concerned for their safety. Deepwater fishing had been new to both Jim and Jill when they first arrived in Alaska from Wyoming. But they had lived off the sea for many years now, and knew the risks.

Quite suddenly, a storm blew in, wind raking the boat, snow sheeting the distance. Fighting the wheel, Blades searched for shelter. Finally he thought it best to overnight at the backside of Saint Lazaria Island, where the boat could find protection from ocean swells and a southeasterly storm.

Unexpectedly, winds began twisting from the opposite direction—southwest, "screaming down off of Mount Edgecumbe." Before long forty-knot gusts pounded the boat, with heavy snow squalls soon following. The change in wind direction left the *Bluebird* exposed and in great peril of being smashed against the rugged island.

Blades knew the danger. Without delay, he fitted Clinton into his survival suit and pulled on his own. The suits, newly repaired, did not have wooden toggles to zipper them tight against water leaking in, but the buoyancy was there to keep them on top. Then he raised the anchor and wheeled the troller away from the rocks.

By the time the boat swung free, Blades had no view beyond the bow—dark and snow made visibility impossible. Riding the rough water, fighting the wind and waves, he could only hope to clear the rocky shoreline.

But *Bluebird*'s thirty-five-horsepower diesel could not summon the power. A few minutes later a huge wave lifted the vessel and smashed her down against shore. The dreaded splintering sound cracked through the turbulence as the hull smacked the rocks. The boat rode up on shore again, opened the hull to water, and slid back down.

Blades grabbed the radio mike. "Mayday! Mayday! Mayday!" he called. "I've hit Lazaria rocks, and I'm sinking." By then the wounded *Bluebird* rode three-story-high waves; seventy-knot winds blasted her side. Yet she struggled to stay afloat.

Coast Guard Air Station Sitka, about twelve miles across Sitka Sound, caught the call. Within minutes, a Sikorsky HH-3F search-and-rescue helicopter rose into the air. As the craft crossed the sound, the weather worsened; snow soon covered the windows, and ice formed along the chopper.

Below, *Bluebird*'s stern now under, the boat rocked on the heavy seas, riding broadside to the thirty-foot waves. Praying his boat would stay afloat, Blades desperately flashed his spotlight to help the aircraft zero in.

In the helicopter, pilot Lieutenant Commander John Whiddon, who later recorded the experience in *Alaska* magazine, and copilot Lieutenant Greg Breithaupt fought the gusting winds and driving snow flurries trying to locate the tiny troller. Finally approaching the area, flight mechanic Carl Saylor spotted the white dot of *Bluebird*. "Pilot . . . I think I see a flashing light."

As the helicopter began turning on descent to three hundred feet, radar contact with Saint Lazaria Island blinked out. What happened? the crew wondered. Then they realized: The helicopter, while leveling off—in the shortest blink—had been blown far off course by the wind! The heavy seas were also moving the sinking troller farther from Saint Lazaria.

Struggling to bank around, the helo returned and hovered above the boat. For reference, the air crew dropped smoke flares—instantly flung away by the wind. The helicopter's floodlights, however, showed what was occurring on the ocean: the tiny broken craft was being tossed like a peanut shell as mountainous waves washed the darkness below, snow veiling the scene.

Blades and his son desperately held on to the dying *Bluebird*, listing and taking on water, waves washing over the deck. The helo crew tried to lower a rescue basket and set it on the vessel, but rigging on the sinking boat flapped in the way. If the basket snagged on the boat, it could take the helicopter down, too.

A sudden strong gust slammed the helicopter and forced it back and down. Whiddon and Breithaupt pulled all the force they could, but the wind drove the helo down, closer to the reaching waves. Just fifteen feet from the sea, the gust slowed, helo energy kicked in, and the chopper shot up again to safety.

After regaining control, Whiddon swung the helo back above the boat. Saylor likened the wind power to a "fan blowing against a paper airplane."

Rescue from the sinking boat proved impossible. Breithaupt radioed down to Blades, "You'll have to get in the water for us to rescue you." He directed them to swim away from the vessel.

Blades wasted no time. He strapped Clinton to his chest and jumped into the thirty-foot seas. Instantly their survival suits filled with icy water, taking their breaths away, numbing the two. Losing strength, they would need help getting into the rescue basket.

Just as the chopper descended to try for a pickup, the wind smashed against the leaning *Bluebird*. From low on one side, the boat mast arced through the air to the other side, missing the dropping helicopter by just four feet.

Jim Blades tried to swim away from the boat, but the power of the waves washed him back. The dying *Bluebird*, pounded by the sea, could take no more and sank beneath the surface, its blazing spotlight following it down. Now, however, the empty water left a clear path for rescue.

Different thoughts darted through Blades's mind as he shivered in the icy sound. Foremost, he wanted to get his son out safely. Then he worried he would die, and his son would have a dead father strapped to him, drifting about in the ocean.

Coast Guard rescue swimmer Jeff Tunks waited above. At the right time, he swung from the chopper on the rescue sling. "When I was on the way down," he said, "I could see the guy, so as soon as I hit the water I unhooked from the sling." Totally free swimming, he no longer had connection with the helicopter above.

Yet once in the rolling waves, Tunks could see nothing. Confused, he did not know which direction to go, so he swam toward the light beaming down from the chopper. Though he shouted to the Bladeses, the roaring storm whipped away his words. When a wave crest rode the victims high, Tunks spotted a reflection off the survival suits from the helo's searchlight, about seventy-five yards away. He swam, struggling, to the Bladeses' position.

As reported in the *Daily Sitka Sentinel*, Tunks, the father of a three-year-old himself, said, "When I saw the kid, that gave me the determination to get them in the basket. The boy showed no emotion. He had complete trust in his father."

But six-year-old Clinton recalled being more active, coughing and spitting up water. He waved his arms to the helicopter when his father did. Several times he fell asleep. He remembered waking up in the water, with the underlights of the helicopter blinking directly above him.

Constantly fighting the gusting winds above, flight mechanic Saylor and radioman Mark Milne hung out the door and called directions to Whiddon, who could not always see what was going on under the aircraft. Copilot Breithaupt, in turn, kept an eye on air speed, altitude, and power gauges. Whiddon absorbed everything, engrossed in keeping a hover over the two victims below and preventing the aircraft from going in. Fuel was running low, too—another worry.

It took four passes over fifteen minutes before Saylor finally lowered a rescue basket into position. Once within reach below, Tunks snared the basket and gathered the survivors together. As he rolled the two into the basket, he heard Jim's teeth chattering. Bucking the winds, rescuers hoisted the two victims into the rocking helicopter. Young Clinton recalled the foam at the end of his survival suit sleeve snagged in the basket rigging as he was lifted up to the helicopter, Carl Saylor and Jim Blades working to free it. And he remembered being rolled into the helicopter, and his father asking, "Are you OK, son?"

But the job was not over.

Now the crew had to pick up Tunks. The helicopter made one, two, three, four passes over the swimmer. On one, wind gusts forced the helicopter from a sixty-foot hover, shooting it into a dive about fifteen feet from the water. "I thought we were going in," Whiddon said.

The situation grew desperate, with disastrous weather, and fuel running low. They couldn't get Tunks out. The weather was so rotten that the helo crew seriously considered throwing a rescue raft into the water for Tunks and leaving, rather than endangering everyone. "Cut ties or everyone would be in dire jeopardy," Saylor said. The crew felt the swimmer would be all right drifting in the raft, waiting out the storm.

Before they could bring themselves to do that, they made one last attempt. On the fifth try, miraculously, Tunks caught the basket and swung himself in. Saylor began hoisting the swimmer. He couldn't do it too fast, for with the violent winds, the basket might flip and hit the helo. Then suddenly another incredible wind gust of sixty knots smashed the helicopter back and left Tunks in a swing seventy-five feet ahead of the craft. Arcing down at terrific speed, the basket crashed with a white explosion through the crest of a wave.

Whiddon recalled the moment to the *Daily Sitka Sentinel*: "We were going backwards at fifty miles an hour when I saw him go through the crest of a wave.

During the worst possible weather, this rescue crew saved Jim Blades and his son when their fishing vessel went down in December 1987.

There was a massive explosion; I thought I killed him."

Tunks was dragged through two more waves, his mask and snorkel ripped away, the helicopter shuddering from each impact. Finally Saylor, working the basket hoist, managed to swing Tunks high and free of the waves. Then they had to wait, the newspaper later reported. "The gyrations of the basket [had] to stop before the crew could reel him in. Hoisting a swinging basket too fast might allow it to crash into the side of the aircraft." Carefully the hoist operator brought the swimmer up. Once in the cabin, Tunks threw up seawater and had trouble keeping his balance. But everyone was in and alive. Anxious moments continued as Widdon headed for Sitka, not sure the chopper could make it back to base. With relief, the aircraft at last touched down on the air station runway.

Back in Sitka, a medical team examined Tunks and the Bladeses, who were treated for minor injuries and soon released from the hospital. The one "member" of the rescue team that emerged seriously wounded was the helicopter. It held out well during the flight, but showed its battering on return. Carl Saylor likened the outside of the helicopter—the airframe—to an empty soda pop can. Crush the can, and then open it back up. Crinkles on the sides mark and weaken the stressed metal. Besides damage to the outside, the main transmission had been badly twisted; a new one had to be purchased from North Carolina.

The Coast Guard crew received several major individual and group awards for countless dangers during this daring rescue. Among them shone the State of Alaska Award for Bravery-Heroism, which Governor Steve Cowper presented at Coast Guard Air Station Sitka.

Jim Blades and his family—now grown to four children—still live outside Sitka in a wilderness area, running a commercial lodge there called Homestead Outfitters.

Once the *Bluebird* went down, Blades never bought another boat. For several years he crewed on fishing vessels, until he began a commercial diving operation of his own. Now, diving from a twenty-four-foot skiff, he harvests such creatures as abalone and sea urchins, mostly for the Asian market. His son, Clint, who recently graduated from home high school, works and lives in Sitka, and is deciding what he wants to do with his life.

Some of the Coast Guard crew scattered to new posts since the rescue; Tunks was stationed in New Orleans, Saylor decided to leave rescue work and transferred to a Coast Guard position in Virginia, and Milne retired.

This event left a profound impression on its participants. For most of the crew, it proved the worst rescue situation they had ever experienced. Considering the wind, cold, water, darkness, and snow, there was every chance all involved—everyone—could have been swallowed by the sea and never seen again. Only skill, training, and a lot of luck kept the episode from becoming a tragedy.

A *Daily Sitka Sentinel* letter to the editor said it all: "Only a combination of these highly trained men's grim determination and divine intervention saved this father and son from sure death in the icy waters. . . ." ★

# LAST VOYAGE OF THE *DORA H.*

## Off Kodiak, 1991

The fifty-three-foot halibut fishing boat *Dora H.* rolled in thirty-five-foot seas, blasted by heavy rain and winds. With thick clouds crowding above, the night grew dark early despite May's longer days. Ship position: 150 miles south of Kodiak Island in the Pacific Ocean, many miles from land.

After working long hours with only a few rests, Captain Mark Worley and crewmen Eric Harvey and Dan Bass were growing rummy. More than halfway through a twenty-four-hour halibut opening, they finally found a few moments of rest and crashed below, catching what sleep they could on the rolling seas.

Crewman Kirk Van Doren, on watch in the wheelhouse at the time, felt exhaustion seep through his bones. Peering into the dim distance and trying to stay alert, he slowly came to realize the *Dora H.* was riding strangely, listing to port. The hold carried thirty thousand pounds of halibut, yes, but wasn't the boat especially low in the water even at that? In spite of the rough seas, Van Doren sensed something was wrong.

Almost in the next moment, a bilge alarm blasted below. Then another. The signals could only mean the vessel floundered in serious trouble. "We took a big one over the bait tent," Van Doren reported, "and the boat did not right itself." He raced to wake Captain Worley and the rest of the crew. No doubt about it, the vessel plowed along unusually low in the seas and was going down.

Desperately bracing at the helm, driving into the waves, trying to keep the ship afloat, Worley told himself the boat was not sinking. After all, the *Dora* had been heavily loaded before, waves had washed the deck, and the boat had lifted back. But this time all efforts failed—the vessel kept going under.

"Let's get the heck out of here," Captain Worley finally shouted. Abandon ship!

Facing darkness outside, rotten weather, still miles from land, and sinking rapidly, the captain radioed a "Mayday" with their location. Both the sideband and the VHF gave off distress calls. Two distant fishing vessels—the F/V *Hornet* and the F/V *Aleutian*—responded, one hearing only ". . . stern is under, pilothouse is filling with water." U.S. Coast Guard watchstanders at Air Station Kodiak, however, caught the message, which ended, "We're in our suits; we're going down." A brief reply told Worley the station was alerted.

Crew members dove for their survival suits. Jumping into his, Bass ripped the neoprene seal around the hood. Now he was in real trouble. "I knew it wasn't working," he said. "I was going to freeze to death in forty-degree water." But he put it on anyway.

While Eric Harvey, a seasoned commercial fisherman, pulled on his suit, he wondered how it would feel to have a boat go down under him. The thought of his new son and his wife flashed to mind. Yet, he had confidence: the Mayday had gone out; Kodiak had responded. Help would be on the way.

Even in the giant seas, the crew felt the boat list and flounder. With the hold full of halibut, the *Dora H.* was sinking "butt first," said Worley. Already water swamped the deck.

Van Doren, rain raking his body, vaulted to the roof of the pilothouse, catching at poles there to keep his balance, and located the new life raft. Bracing against a roll, he broke through the plywood packing with his hands, only to find metal bands circling the packet. In one motion, he jerked out his halibut-heading knife and cut through the bands. As he prepared to lower the packet, struggling to hold on, a huge wave washed over the roof and pulled the raft from his grip.

No time to think. He dove for the old life raft, struggling to release it. He couldn't free it from its bracket.

Captain Worley hurried up, shouting that water splashed waist deep in the galley. The new raft, barely visible in the night, washed free from the sinking stern. Heads turned to the package, now drifting twenty feet off the boat, fast disappearing in the constant roll. Their lifeline! Their only choice—jump in, swim to it.

Harvey, riding with the waves, stroking expertly, struggled to the packaged raft. Bass, clad in pajama tops and pants, jumped in, and felt the icy sea leak through his survival suit, filling it with numbing water. Yet he swam, and reached the package, too. Other crew followed. What to do with the encased raft? Finally Harvey shouted, "I have the painter line." Everyone screamed, "Pull!" Harvey jerked, yanking nearly 150 feet of line until the raft finally, blessedly, ballooned out.

"That was the first big moment of joy," said Bass, "when that thing went poof, whir, and it inflated."

One at a time, the four men scrambled into the shelter of the domed, windowed raft. They watched the *Dora H.* lose its battle, tipping back farther, then sliding under the surface.

In their anxiety to jump ship, no one had remembered to grab the handheld emergency locator unit. Rescue parties had only a general idea of their position

Before the disaster, the *Dora H.* anchors off Montague Island, Alaska, during the 1990 summer season.

from the Mayday. The raft drifted, darkness all around, the safety of land a long way distant, and nothing but moving, ever-changing ocean surrounding them. Spotting a tiny raft under such conditions seemed laughable.

One mistake, however, proved valuable. Bass, overtired on the boat, "had forgotten to turn off the battery-operated strobe lights on the ten-foot fishing flagpoles," according to the *Kodiak Daily Mirror.* When the *Dora H.* sank—in about fifteen minutes' time—the blinking lighted strobes lifted off the vessel and drifted near the raft, offering a beacon of their own.

Huddling inside, the men talked of their families and the *Dora H.* Finally fumbling around, they found the stored emergency food and dug in. "But it was awful stuff. Dried food," Worley said. "The only thing good were the jelly beans."

The seas thundered around them, disheartening the survivors. Pitch black inside the raft, the men could distinguish things only by feel. Light of some kind—anything—would give substance to the fragile world around them. More fumbling in the dark, and someone found a glo stick and located the lifesaving kit.

No sooner was this done than a crushing wave broke through the raft's Velcro door fastener and the sea plunged in, soaking the crew, tumbling items inside and washing others out the door. The relentless ocean left the victims with a pint can of fresh water, a flashlight, and half an oar.

The heaving sea pounded at the men. Each time they heard a deep rumble, a wave would lift the raft up thirty-five feet, then plunge it down again, like heavy surf on a beach. With the wave came icy water, surging inside, splashing around.

Finally the men took turns sitting, straddling the door inside and out, paddling with the half oar, hoping in some way to direct the raft downwind and keep the water from flooding in. They all spent time during those long hours bailing out, and wondering if anyone would come.

So there they were, the tiny craft in darkness, pelted with rain, no locator beacon, riding icy thirty-five-foot waves. Next stop south, the Hawaiian Islands, was a couple thousand miles away.

Meanwhile, earlier, command at Air Station Kodiak had caught the Mayday. Seven minutes after midnight, an H-3 Rescue 1467 helicopter responded, taking off in solid overcast with rain, fog, snow flurries, and total darkness. The crew consisted of pilot (Clifford) Keith Comer in the right seat, copilot Bob Yerex, swimmer Gary Strebe, and, working the hoist, navigator Dave Schron and flight mechanic Jeff Waite.

In support of the rescue, officials at the Kodiak station routinely launched a Coast Guard C-130 to shadow the helicopter and assist with navigation and weather data. This fixed-wing aircraft proved the baby-sitter, the "warm fuzzy" that flew from three hundred to five hundred feet above the water to keep an eye on everything.

Into the flight, the helicopter's LORAN C (long-range navigational system) became inoperative, and OMEGA (the aircraft positioning device) began emitting wrong longitudinal readings. To add more difficulties, the radar failed, and Comer turned it off. At times, the helicopter flew blind.

Powerful and gusting winds caused severe turbulence—so much so that copilot Yerex grew violently ill, while pilot Comer kept his hand on the stick. A Coast Guard Academy man with seventeen years in the sky, Comer had flown numerous rescues before.

While the chopper plowed toward the Mayday position, Comer had a decision to make: If they found the raft, should he allow the swimmer into the ocean in the dark, in such weather? Once on the water and released from the cable, the swimmer moved free, on his own—a terribly risky setup. Comer put off the question until, and if, they arrived on the scene.

As the helicopter approached the general area, trying to pinpoint any light source that might be the raft, it picked up contact with scattered fishing vessels.

Compounding these sightings were the halibut strobes: Fishermen attached strobe lights to either end of the halibut sets on the ocean surface for ease in finding the nets.

Copilot Yerex's job in the left seat was as safety pilot—monitoring fuel, passing on information, maintaining a calm mood, watching the weather, checking power. Using night-vision goggles, Yerex finally spotted a strobe that shone slightly different. "That's it," he said with relief. Three hours after the *Dora H.* went down, the chopper beamed a searchlight onto the tiny raft.

The helicopter began circling, losing altitude, approaching for a hover. Just as the aircraft positioned itself, an extreme downdraft struck. Both pilots fought to hold altitude, but the wind thrust the aircraft down, down to within fifteen feet of the water.

Way too dangerous. The chopper crew was prepared for the differing wave heights, twenty, maybe thirty feet. It was that lone rogue wave, that fifty-footer that either built by itself, or combined with another wave, that could be the killer. Surging along, this rogue wave could surprise the helicopter and slap it out of the sky. As the helicopter hovered just fifteen feet above the water, a wave higher than the chopper cabin rolled toward them.

Pilot Comer felt they might go in then, despite desperate attempts to pull the chopper up. By the grace of God, Yerex remembered thinking, they finally got a response and the chopper forced a slow, labored climb away from the clutch of that monster wave. Relief in the cabin was palpable.

With some of the H-3's systems not reacting properly, the helicopter had difficulty establishing a stable hover over the raft, and the crew could not rely on the instruments. A few were simply turned off. The situation was tough: pitch dark, seas at forty feet, icy thirty-five-degree water, winds gusting at forty to fifty-five knots. This meant that, except for flares on the water, and a fishing vessel in the distance for reference, the pilot "spent the next fifty minutes in a manual night-over-water hover, with no other external clue," according to a Coast Guard account.

Pilot Comer made a decision: the Coast Guard would continue. Swimmer Gary Strebe was lowered on a cable to the water—the first time Air Station Kodiak had used a rescue swimmer. Wind and water actions made tricky business of the drop because of wave height.

"Sometimes the swimmer was fifteen feet under the aircraft, sometimes maybe eighty feet," Yerex said. Above, Dave Schron kept a handheld Aldis light shining down on the raft to give Strebe direction.

Just as Strebe released from the sling below, the swell dropped, and so did Strebe. The cable jerked, ripping the swimmer's mask and snorkel from his face.

Skipper Mark Worley working aboard the *Golden Chalice*
in Juneau's downtown harbor, April 1999.

Once in the water, Strebe rolled for a second, then finally gave an "OK" signal, and swam to the raft.

When Strebe stuck his face through the door, hoping to lighten the situation, he said, "This isn't a drill." He asked if everyone was inside, and then told them what would happen. Because the chopper was running low on fuel, the rescue might abort. He made radio contact with the aircraft and got word to continue with the rescue.

Above, the helicopter bobbed up and down in the wind, altitude anywhere from twenty-five to seventy-five feet from the waves. At one point, the chopper settled to ten feet above the sea, and hoist operator Dave Schron's yell, "UP—UP—UP—you're descending!" saved the helo from crashing into the water.

Meanwhile the hoist basket was lowered and the rescues began, one at a time. First, Strebe guided Dan Bass, who was whipped away and up. As he finally rolled into the helicopter above, crawled forward, and lay on the floor, he gave a grateful, "Yes, yes, yes, yes, yes."

Below, the heavy metal basket swung wildly under the aircraft and out, making it difficult to manage. Hoist operator Jeff Waite "played the hoist like a yo-yo" while Dave Schron tried to stabilize the cable from above. On one occasion, Schron knelt, one hand on the cable. He turned to grab the Aldis lamp, and a wave caught the full basket below and snapped the cable back. The upper cable struck Schron's helmet, forcing it—along with his head—into the helicopter's door frame. The blow hit so violently, the pilots heard the crack in the cockpit, and Schron "saw stars" for a moment.

Once Schron had hoisted Bass into the chopper, Eric Harvey went next. As Strebe stuck his head in the raft for another man, Van Doren and Worley were arguing who would go next. "One of you make up your mind," Strebe shouted over the wind. Worley remained behind while Van Doren was lifted into the chopper.

By the time Strebe rolled Worley into the basket below, the swimmer felt his muscles giving out and knew he'd reached the end of his strength. He was well aware that fuel ran low, too. Rather than send the fisherman up and wait for another hoist, Strebe snapped his D ring to the basket and rode up with the survivor. Once in the aircraft, he became sick from all the seawater he had swallowed.

The helicopter crew grew elated when they heard Waite say over the intercom, "He's [Strebe] in the basket; we have them both." The pilot remembered great relief at hearing everyone was finally hauled on board, and he mentally tipped his hat to the crew in back. "They maintained maturity and confidence. They kept their cool," he said. "A team effort, along with some luck."

Physically exhausted, Comer did not know if he could last the flight back. He'd spent hours in the pilot seat, stiff hands gripping the controls, fighting winds, holding position, alert to every change, ultimately responsible for everyone. Exhausting. For the moment, he relaxed and let Yerex take them all back.

The helicopter raced for Kodiak, with worries whether the fuel would last. While in flight, the crew checked the survivors, stripped off their wet clothes, and wrapped them in wool blankets and hypothermia bags. Six and one-half hours after takeoff, the helicopter touched down on the Kodiak runway. Following examinations at the Kodiak hospital, doctors released all the *Dora H.* crew in good shape.

Coast Guardsman Dave Schron might have been the only seriously injured member of the rescue, except for wearing his helmet. He almost hadn't.

As it happened, the helicopter crew flew a training flight before the rescue. Schron noticed something wrong with his ICS (internal communications system), the microphone on his helmet. Since the men wear the same helmet all the time, he put his aside and planned only on wearing a headset should he have to go out. When the Mayday came in, swimmer Strebe told Schron to use his helmet, since swimmers wore only snorkel and mask in the water. Schron donned Strebe's helmet, which protected him when the cable snapped his head against the helicopter door frame. Otherwise, he could have been seriously injured, if not killed.

Strangely, that same evening, some twelve hundred miles southeast, Worley's wife, Lisa Newland, deep in comfortable sleep at home in Gig Harbor, Washington, woke in the middle of the night, calling Mark's name. Some inner sense of danger woke her.

The Coast Guard crew was hailed for a successful rescue. For their outstanding actions during this rescue, the helicopter crew received the State of Alaska Award for Bravery-Heroism, given in Anchorage on October 16, 1992, by Governor Walter Hickel. The Naval Helicopter Association also honored the crew in March of 1992.

Captain Mark Worley never found out what brought the *Dora H.* down. The men had worked so hard on getting her in shape. "Maybe she lost a plank in the hull" was his educated guess.

Like getting back on a horse after being thrown off, Worley purchased a fifty-eight-foot fishing boat, the *Golden Chalice*, a month after losing the *Dora H.* With Van Dorn along, Worley had a successful first fishing trip out, packing twenty thousand pounds of halibut on deck. Yet the load was so heavy, the *Chalice* started listing.

Oh no, Worley told himself, not again! However, nothing proved wrong with the sturdy ship, and careful handling brought it safely into port.

Through the years after the rescue, the crews of the fishing boat and the helicopter scattered. Living in Washington with his family during the winter, Worley captains his *Golden Chalice* in Alaska waters during the fishing season, Van Doren continues commercial fishing out of Homer, Harvey joined the Eagle River Fire Department, and Bass's whereabouts are unknown.

Coast Guard members transferred to other stations in the United States— San Diego, Michigan, Georgia—while Yerex presently copilots out of Sitka in Alaska. After twenty years in the service, pilot Keith Comer retired in the East and currently works on a master's degree. "I've been on a lot of rescues," Comer said, "and I wanted to use my skills in other areas. Besides, after rescue work, I've always felt I've used up eight of my nine lives. I didn't want to press my luck."

Before his rescue from the *Dora H.*, Worley said, he sometimes harbored a love/hate relationship with the Coast Guard; fishermen don't always feel in tune with all the rules of the sea enforced by the Guard. But they respect it, too. After the rescue, Worley said, "Kodiak especially has great training, and they do the most amazing rescues. We were blessed with the best pilot. What they all do is incredible, amazing." Kirk Van Dorn echoed the same sentiments. "Fishermen get paid a lot for their jobs. Coast Guard people don't get paid very much, but they put their lives on the line. I have total respect for them." ★

★

# "HE GAVE HIS LIFE TO SAVE A FRIEND . . ."

## Nome, 1984

After end-of-week celebrating Friday night, Nome, Alaska, held that early Saturday morning hush in 1984. At 4:15 A.M., most residents slept, and few cars cruised the streets. With September shifting into winter, darkness blanketed the town.

Behind Washington Olanna's home on East Fourth Avenue stood a two-room, single-story wood structure. This residence served as the home of Betty Jean Olanna, daughter of Washington, where she lived with her son, Darin, ten, and her daughter, Penny, six. At the time, Betty was not in Nome, having flown to Anchorage for a shopping weekend.

With his mother gone earlier on Friday, Darin visited his grandfather Washington while Penny stayed nearby with her Uncle Jake. Late in the day two adult sisters, JoAnne, twenty-one, and Gloria Pootoogooluk, eighteen, flew in from Shishmaref to spend the weekend and see friends, and agreed to stay with the children for a few days in Betty's house. Since Darin enjoyed a friendly relationship with his sister, he hurried over to Uncle Jake's and brought Penny home, ready to include her in any excitement. Penny and Darin spent the early evening playing outside, riding bikes.

After going out to Milano's for a pizza dinner later, then stopping at several stores for groceries and beer, everyone returned home. When Darin's young cousin, Alfred Kiyutelluk, nine, played over for a while, he asked to spend the night—only the second time Alfred had slept over. Alfred called his mother for permission.

Soon after, JoAnne left for the evening, and Darin, Alfred, Gloria, and Penny watched the movie *Popeye* on television. Darin kept his own fold-up cot next to the kitchen empty for JoAnne's use when she came back. A while later, JoAnne returned to the house and the older girls did some drinking together. Darin and Alfred settled on the bedroom floor with sleeping gear and watched TV until they fell asleep. Finally, Gloria retired to Betty's big bed in the bedroom with Penny. JoAnne took the cot.

About 4:30 in the morning, the crackling of fire or something falling woke Darin; smoke and flames quickly made him alert. Momentarily dazed, he

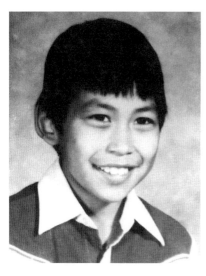

Darin Olanna.

reached over and shook Alfred. Both of them felt the heat and watched in stunned silence for a second while the fire grew in the small house. Already flames whipped up the walls toward the ceiling, and clouds of smoke boiled through the room. In the dry weather, the wood structure burned quickly.

Through the roar of the blaze, the boys heard what sounded like screaming from outside. Darin and Alfred sprang up shouting, alerting the other people in the house. Pieces of fire fell on Alfred, and he rolled on the floor to put out the flames.

Difficulty breathing in the smoky interior awoke Penny. She caught sounds from the television, until suddenly the set exploded. Frantically she looked around. Familiar with the house, she knew to go to the door, but a floor fire that reached to her knees blocked the way. She jumped over it and other little fires at her feet.

Both Alfred and Darin pushed at JoAnne, face down on the cot, shaking her, trying to get her up. Nothing worked. Through the smoke, the noise, the confusion, Penny thought she remembered hearing JoAnne screaming. Finally Alfred, now burned on his feet, face, and hands, grabbed Penny and dragged her from the building into the darkness outside.

Accounts vary, but Penny thought Darin followed them outside and stood next to her in the dark. Then in a second she felt him rush back inside for another try at JoAnne. Others said Darin never left the house, desperately working inside to rouse JoAnne to get her moving.

Eighteen-year-old Gloria stood just outside the flaming structure, crying, screaming, and jumping around in the dark. Alfred, himself seriously injured, tried stumbling back inside to see about Darin, but the whole structure blazed by then, smoke pouring out the windows, intense heat driving him back.

Upset and crying, Penny and Alfred ran to their Uncle Jake's house near the playground, where he phoned 911 and then took the children to the hospital.

Darin could have dashed out the door with Alfred, or stayed outside, but he remained behind, trying urgently to help the older girl, JoAnne, to safety. Possibly due to her drinking, Darin had difficulty prodding her awake, and escape time—even those few feet to safety outdoors—narrowed. Darin must have felt his efforts useless, for he finally swung around and made one urgent attempt to bolt outside. But because of the churning smoke and fiery heat, the fire caught him. Nome volunteer firemen later discovered his body inside, face down, a few feet from the front door.

Forensic reports stated Darin and JoAnne both died in the fire, and as a result of the fire. The residence blazed hot and fast, with little of the structure remaining: total burn time until the fire was extinguished was about twenty minutes. Officials immediately medevacced young Alfred to the Alaska Native Medical Center in Anchorage for care, and notified Betty Olanna in Anchorage, who immediately flew home. Several days later, Betty Olanna buried her son Darin next to his grandmother's grave in Nome. Gloria returned to Shishmaref.

For his unselfish act in attempting to save the life of JoAnne Pootoogooluk, Darin Olanna received the State of Alaska Award for Bravery-Heroism posthumously, accepted by his mother. Alfred Kiyutelluk also received a commendation. The state fire marshal, Sylvester Neal, delivered the awards in Nome before a PTA meeting in January 1985.

The tragedy might have ended there—two accidental deaths in an intense fire, the funerals, the grieving, the awards, the memories long to live in relatives' minds. But fire inspectors, well experienced with all types of blazes, felt uneasy. Too many questions remained. The first to be answered was "how."

When fire examiners checked the scene, they detected little indication that the fire broke out from expected, random causes: the oil stove in the kitchen area did not leak; the stove burner pot did not show signs of overheating; the chimney was not plugged; boxes near the stove had not ignited; electrical appliances were not faulty. They were able to eliminate all these accidental factors.

Yet the kitchen area showed heavy scorching across the cabinets and ceiling. Plastic covering the windows in the building quickly melted, allowing air to enter and fan the flames. Sills revealed deep charring—especially one window directly over the cot where JoAnne slept.

Once workers cleared away debris, it appeared the fire started low and raged hot and fast. Burn patterns—a back-and-forth distribution—seemed consistent with use of an accelerant such as gas or diesel fuel, which radiated from the bedroom entrance into the kitchen area. Gathering all the facts, an investigator from Fairbanks said, "This fire was rapid building and extremely fast, indicating and leading this officer to believe it was intentionally set." Soon after the initial investigation, the Nome Police Department had little choice but to consider arson.

The next question to be answered was "who."

For several days following the fire, police officers interviewed those directly involved—Gloria, Alfred, and Penny. Nothing improper surfaced. And no one saw strangers earlier that evening loitering around the Olanna house. The police then expanded the interviews to bartenders, neighbors, and friends who knew the Pootoogooluk sisters. Since JoAnne was the fatality, police concentrated on her contacts before the fire—where she went, whom she spoke to. Everyone said that except for her drinking, for the most part she conveyed a happy mood. No particular problems emerged.

Weeks into the investigation, an interview with a neighbor disclosed that on that particular Saturday morning, after being jarred awake by screaming, the neighbor reported seeing the outline of a female jumping around in front of the burning house, and hearing her holler in a confused manner, shouting something like "JoAnne, JoAnne, I love you . . . I'm sorry I did it . . . God, please forgive me." Other neighbors heard similar words, too.

When police further interviewed a friend of Gloria's, it appeared Gloria was having trouble with a boyfriend and had been depressed. The night of the fire, Gloria phoned her friend and said, "Don't be surprised if something happens to me."

By that time enough evidence existed to raise questions about Gloria's involvement in the fire, and police flew her in from Shishmaref for an interview. After lengthy questioning, the young girl broke down and confessed to starting the fire. It seems Gloria went outside in the wee hours of that Saturday morning, filled a plastic jug with gasoline, and brought it back into the house, spilling the contents around boxes in the kitchen. She then took paper tissues, lit them with a cigarette lighter, and tossed them on the gasoline.

The last question to be answered was "why?"

Already Gloria's boyfriend played a prominent role in the police picture. The two were breaking up, and Gloria felt angry at herself for being taken in by him. Plus the drinking and depression gave her suicidal ideas. She stated she wanted to hurt herself, but had no intention of harming anyone else. She acted impulsively and had not thought things through.

Following a grand jury indictment, authorities charged Gloria with arson and two counts of second-degree murder for her ". . . extreme indifference to the value of human life. . . . " After a psychological evaluation in Anchorage, troopers returned her to the Nome Correctional Facility. Gloria served her term and is out today, living a quiet life.

After the blaze, relatives in Shishmaref took little Penny Olanna to live with them for several years. For months, fiery dreams haunted Penny, and she slept with her tights or jeans on, and grew especially cautious of matches.

Eventually the images faded, although even today a detail, or a "what if," can bring back that traumatic morning when she was only six. One memory was the fact that a large container of drinking water stood by the house entrance. If she had overturned it into the house, it might have made a difference by extinguishing some of the flames.

Today Penny has completed several years of schooling at Linfield College in Oregon, studying to become a social worker. Since she and Darin had a caring relationship in younger years, she still misses him. "I used to look up to him and follow him around," she said, "and he used to look after me."

Alfred Kiyutelluk is now grown. After periodically living and working in Oregon and Seattle—most currently for the Glacier Fish Company—he returned to Shishmaref. A member of the National Guard, he enjoys hunting, fishing, and working.

And of course even today Betty Olanna feels sad when remembering her young son. The same year Darin died, Betty gave birth to another child whom she named Darin, after her lost boy.

The September 1984 house fire in Nome that took the life of ten-year-old Darin Olanna should never have happened. By rights, Darin should be a grown man today. Though a criminal act set the house fire in motion, it does not lessen the bravery of the young boy who courageously tried to help another and ended giving up his own life.

A few weeks after the blaze in 1984, Darin's fourth-grade class wrote letters to the *Nome Nugget* newspaper. School classmates, as well as family, felt the loss of Darin, who was well liked. In the tribute, class members said, "Darin loved life. He loved his family . . . his friends. He gave his life to save a friend." ★

★

# NO SECOND CHANCE

### Fairbanks, 1972

Thirteen-year-old Jeffrey Stone, son of Army Staff Sergeant J. M. Stone, huddled in a jacket and hurried down a quiet residential street on Fort Wainwright Military Reservation in January 1972. The base abutted Fairbanks to the east; Army personnel worked and lived on the grounds. Jeffrey delivered the *Fairbanks Daily News-Miner* on his paper route.

Although the hour had not yet reached 4:00 P.M., dark and cold already blanketed the town—a bitter minus twenty degrees just then—with the night promising even harsher weather. Low temperatures pulled moisture from the air, leaving everything—inside and out—tinder dry.

In spite of the darkness, as Jeffrey passed one of the housing units, he spotted intense smoke pouring from a window. Perhaps seeing light inside, Jeffrey ran up the walk to the building and pounded on the door, trying to alert someone. "Anybody home?" he shouted.

Receiving no response and finding the door locked, Jeffrey smashed his fist through the glass above the handle, reached in, and opened the lock. A cloud of smoke and heat funneled out as the glass broke away, and Jeffrey forced his way in. Pushing through the doorway, he shouted over and over to see if anyone was there, not sure if he heard something through the crackling noise. Nevertheless, he had to be sure, and he groped farther into the smoke.

Jeffrey hunched low, peering into the darkness, coughing and calling. He held up an arm to protect his face as he searched another room. By now smoke swirled around him, bringing tears that streamed down his cheeks. Finally, miraculously, he either heard something or distinguished the shadows of two scared children—ages three and four perhaps. They huddled in the dining room area, whimpering. Without hesitation, Jeffrey grabbed the two, groggy from the smoke, and pulled them along, dragging them outside. He shook one, forcing attention, asking if anyone else was inside. "The baby," they answered, "upstairs." No sign of parents around.

Jeffrey whirled about and entered the quarters again. By now flames, set free in the dry air, raged up the stairway, creating a deep, roaring noise. He staggered to the stairs, where the inferno stopped him. His eyes burned; he couldn't see.

With each breath he sucked in heavy smoke, hacking constantly; heat blasted his skin and singed his hair, beating him back.

The wall of fire turned Jeffrey away. But he knew there was a child up there—he had to try again.

Steeling himself, Jeffrey bent low and lunged forward, coughing, trying to break through the flames. The blast drove him back. He tried yet again. The heat and fire raged furiously, the blaze intense. In despair, he knew he would never get through.

Young hero Jeffrey Stone battled a fire to save two small children.

By then the fire department engine had screeched to a halt outside near a gathering crowd. Attention turned quickly to the young children—Carlos and Charmane Dixon—who, once in the fresh air, began to revive. An ambulance crew sped Jeffrey and the two survivors to Bassett Army Hospital. According to a medical team at the hospital, firemen later located the lone infant upstairs, dead from smoke inhalation.

Doctors treated Stone for cuts on his arms, inflicted when he broke the door window. After his release from the hospital, Jeffrey delivered the *Fairbanks Daily News-Miner* to the rest of his customers. The newspaper might have been a little late that night, but Jeffrey had a good excuse and no one complained.

The commander of Fort Wainwright, General Charles Hall, recommended Jeffrey for the heroism medal since the Army had no specific award for such valor. The state agreed.

For his unselfish and valorous act, Governor William Egan presented the State of Alaska Award for Bravery-Heroism to Jeffrey Stone at a ceremony in Juneau in late June 1972. The citation read, in part, "for his great courage in the face of a raging fire, and for his unselfish action at the risk of his own life to save others."

Newspaper coverage of this heroism proved sparse, as were letters or notes on a paper trail. Articles gave little mention of the victim's parents, Sergeant and Mrs. Charles Dixon, why the children were left alone, or any information thereafter. Due to a military base fire, plus changes in base and state schools at the time, yearbook information and photos have disappeared. And because of Stone's common last name, locating him on the Internet proved an impossible task. Many details of this rescue remain a mystery. ★

Hatchet in hand, a despairing Lancaster hopelessly walks away
from the coach engulfed in flames.

★ 4 ★

# VEHICLE RESCUES

One of the likeliest places an average citizen might be called upon to give aid is on the highway. In the two stories in this section, average people make remarkable efforts to assist their fellow travelers. In one tale, a father driving home from work pulls a woman from her burning car, saving her at great risk to himself. In the other story, two soldiers who lingered over a fishing spot and a truck driver passing through struggle together trying to save a driver trapped in a burning tour bus. The memories of that event will be with them forever.

★

# FROM BEAUTIFUL DAY · · ·
# TO NIGHTMARE

### Near Talkeetna, 1993

Interior Alaska was experiencing a perfect July day in 1993, warm and sunny. As the afternoon advanced, however, events moved toward a tragic evening.

Truck driver Tom Burgess had delivered a freight load to Anchorage earlier. He began the long journey driving his tractor-trailer along the forested Parks Highway, returning north to his home base in Fairbanks.

Far up the highway heading south toward Anchorage, Fort Richardson Army Sergeant David Lancaster and his vacationing army friend, Robert Brantley, completed a thousand-mile camping trip around Interior Alaska. About Mile 106 of the Parks Highway, they stopped to fish for pink salmon in Rabideux Creek.

Working up an appetite, the two hopped in the Jeep and drove ten miles down the road to a restaurant. After eating, they could have continued on and made an early arrival in Anchorage. The July sun, however, shone bright and warm, and daylight lasted for many more hours. They also could have continued on south and stopped at another stream for fishing along the way.

Instead, they chose to backtrack north to Mile 106 and fish a few more hours at the very spot they'd left earlier on Rabideux Creek.

At the same time the two army buddies fished and truck driver Burgess headed north, farther up on the Parks Highway sixteen-year-old Stephen Smith traveled north in a red, full-size Ford pickup. Smith, a well-liked guitar player and cross-country skier, was one of the first kids in his age group in the Talkeetna area to earn a driver's license. This trip was a favor, giving a lift to fifteen-year-old twins Graham and Simon Lee, who were on the way to visit their mother at Trapper Creek. Also in the truck, twelve-year-old Jason Link rode along for fun.

Farther up on the same remote birch-wooded highway, a forty-foot Alaska Sightseeing Cruise West motorcoach, driven by thirty-four-year-old Mike Rogers, headed south, carrying fifteen tourists toward Anchorage after a trip to Denali Park. Rogers, a veteran school bus and tour driver, enjoyed entertaining his passengers, and friends referred to him as "the Anchorage Encyclopedia" because of his knowledge of the area.

Directly behind the driver sat Charles Leipzig of Wisconsin; Leipzig's wife, Dana, across the aisle.

Charging around a wide corner in the southbound lane of the highway in a "no passing zone," motorcoach driver Rogers came upon the red Ford truck; it had drifted into the southbound lane. Instinctively, Rogers swerved the coach left into the northbound lane to avoid a collision. At that instant, the Ford truck also veered to the northbound lane to miss the motorcoach.

Rogers screamed. Behind him, Leipzig leaped up from his seat in time to see the Ford hit center on the coach with a terrific crash, the bus's windshield webbing into a million pieces.

With the impact, the bus and truck locked. In a shrieking cloud of gravel and metal particles, the slamming force carried the vehicles south for 110 feet. The mass finally skidded to the side and shuddered to a stop on the shoulder. The four young boys in the truck died instantly.

While fishing on Rabideux Creek, Lancaster and Brantley heard this heart-stopping "*boom!* and screeching metal" not far away near the highway. Because the two had been studying maps and were both experienced soldiers, they first thought they had strayed into a military zone; perhaps the Army had overshot a target. The men dropped their gear; Lancaster picked up a first-aid kit from the Jeep, Brantley grabbed his camera, and they scrambled up the bank.

Facing them loomed a sight few want to remember: the pickup truck, now afire, locked tightly against the huge tour bus, with several bodies close by. Gasoline from the truck dripped out, feeding a fire under the wreckage. From the bus, cries for help called through the air. The soldiers ran forward.

Since the crash took place in a remote wilderness region, miles from civilization, there was no house or store close by, no phone booth where help could be summoned immediately. That meant hands-on rescue right now; they had to do what had to be done.

Inside the bus, once everything settled after the collision, Charles Leipzig picked himself up and then shook Rogers's shoulder, but there was no response—the driver was unconscious. Leipzip's wife had been thrown against the stair railing and under it, landing on the floor. When Charles reached for her, she said, "Don't touch me—my leg's broken." Leipzig climbed out the window and, along with two men, helped others exit.

Returning inside the bus, Charles gathered up his wife as best he could and handed her out the window. He then stretched her out on the road, but the highway surface, heated by the eighty-five-degree sunshine, proved

The fire in the coach was eventually put out.

uncomfortably hot. Finally he dragged her along the ground behind the bus to the side of the road.

Afraid the whole wreckage might explode momentarily, rescuers Brantley and Lancaster nevertheless assisted people out and away from the smoking mass. They helped Dana Leipzig down from the window, and Lancaster threw his first-aid kit at another woman climbing out with a bleeding face. Screams brought Lancaster to the Ford truck; a woman had been hurled from the bus onto the bodies thrown from the pickup, and he pulled her away from the fiery wreckage. She asked about the driver, "Mike—is he all right?"

Lancaster and Brantley jumped in the bus through a front hole and found the driver, Mike Rogers, slumped over the driving wheel, coming back to his senses. The force of the collision had rammed the entire instrument panel into his lap. "Seat belt," he managed. "Ankle." The rescuers undid his seat belt and tried pulling the driver free, but metal pinned his leg to the bus. The men figured Rogers had slammed on the brake, and the impact molded the bus around his leg.

"Help me," the driver pleaded. Through the chaos, Lancaster spoke into the driver's ear, "You're going to be all right, buddy, don't worry."

By then, Lancaster felt the heat of the fire spread, saw the front bus tire in flames. Choking black smoke billowed into the air. The two men tried to heft the driver straight up and out but failed—the leg was firmly caught. They pried at the leg, pulled it in different directions, trying to work it free, but it would not give.

"Mike," Lancaster repeated, "I'm going to get you out of here. Hold on, Mike, we'll get you out."

Brantley kept working at the leg too, fighting the heat, the growing flames. At one point, Lancaster spotted a cooler in the back of the bus and ran to that, hoping to find something wet, but the container proved empty. At another moment, he spotted someone using a fire extinguisher outside on the wrecked truck. Lancaster screamed to use it on the driver; he jumped from the bus, grabbed the extinguisher, but by then nothing remained.

The two rescuers thought to cut Rogers's foot off and save the man, but they believed his calf might be caught too. And the bus—it could explode at any second. All this reasoning sped through their minds, while chaos and fire raged around them. There simply was not enough time.

When near Rogers, Lancaster spoke to him, "Hold on, Mike. We'll get you out," while the driver pleaded, "Help me."

By then others had reached the scene, among them truck driver Tom Burgess. His first reaction was to stay out of the way and let emergency people take care of their business. But then he realized EMTs hadn't arrived yet, so he sprang to help. An elderly man boosted him through a rear bus window, and Burgess tried to free Rogers too, repeating Lancaster's words, "We'll get you out. Hold on."

The flames licked up the bus, igniting the window seals, dripping hot rubber down. The tinted glass windows began bubbling. Heat burned at the skin while the acrid black smoke clawed at the throat. All around them the roar of consuming flames urged them to hurry. Desperately trying to protect the driver, Brantley broke a seat free and shielded the driver with that, while Lancaster kept tugging at Rogers's leg. It would not budge.

The rescuers made a quick decision for Burgess to try and pull the bus away from the truck. Burgess and Brantley jumped outside and attached a heavy chain to the tractor-trailer, but the bus would not shift. Back and forth they worked, hitching one spot, then another, trying to free the coach.

"There wasn't a whole lot of time. I couldn't move the bus. It was too heavy and I was too light," said Burgess.

Then they thought to pull the truck away from the bus. Hitching the chain to his tractor-trailer and to the Ford, Burgess succeeded in dragging the burning truck about fifty yards away from the bus. "When they did finally manage to break the two vehicles apart," the *Anchorage Daily News* reported, "a gush of air only sent the flames higher." The effort proved in vain.

Lancaster continued working with Rogers on the bus. He spoke to the driver, reassuring him. "Hold on, Mike."

Nearly panicked by the urgency, Lancaster jumped from the coach, broke his way through a watching crowd, and dashed to his Jeep. He wrapped a towel around his head for protection and grabbed an ax. Dashing back, he began hacking at the outside of the bus, despite the intense heat. Clearing enough away, he managed to see the driver's foot inside pinned by a piece of metal. Rogers leaned out of the bus as far as he could, trying to avoid the choking smoke. Lancaster bolted around to reenter the bus. "I tried to get back on the bus again, but it was just too hot," he said.

In total grief and frustration, the rescuers stood outside, watched, and listened to the driver's cries, until there were no more sounds.

"Without having the tools there," Burgess said, his voice low, "or the equipment to pry him loose, I don't know what else a guy could have done."

First word of the accident came through earlier from a worker in a store at Mile 115 on the Parks Highway. "Somebody came in and said I better call the troopers fast," reported employee Zona Devon. "'There's a real bad crash on the highway.'"

Both truck and bus were balls of flame by the time the ambulance from Talkeetna arrived. Then other vehicles, from Trapper Creek, Houston, and Willow reached the scene, their medics treating the injured at a roadside gravel pit. Soon a forestry helicopter and a lifeguard helicopter from Providence Hospital landed nearby. They loaded and ferried injured tourists to Valley Hospital in Palmer and to Anchorage. After treatment, doctors released most patients by midnight. Three victims remained in hospitals for further care.

Dana Leipzig continued in the Providence Hospital, where doctors inserted a rod in her broken leg. The Alaska Sightseeing Cruise West company brought her two sons to Alaska and hosted them on a class-A tour while their mother recuperated. She remained there for nine days, until the West company flew the family home.

Lancaster, Brantley, and Burgess agonized that evening, utterly depressed at not saving Mike Rogers's life. Medics brought them to Talkeetna, where a trauma staff—part of the emergency medical team—insisted on counseling the three men. "It helped a lot to let all the feelings out and try to deal with it," Burgess said. "The part I'll never forget is the screams from the driver, and knowing I couldn't do anything," he went on. "That's the part I'll have to live with forever."

Burgess felt badly about the young boys dying. Having talked to Rogers, however, while he was alive—even that short time on the bus—brought the driver's death all the closer, more personal and disturbing. Lancaster also felt that association. In a way, he still misses Rogers, as if he had been a close friend.

This is a current photo of Tom Burgess, who quickly stepped
in to help during the Parks Highway tragedy.

That brief, live connection was more "profound and intense" than he could have imagined. Brantley shared those feelings as well.

The three rescuers went over events in their minds many times after the crash, haunted by what might have been. "What if . . ." was the question they asked themselves; what if they had had more equipment, what if they'd done this first, or that—maybe they could have saved Rogers's life.

Yet, the men could not have done more. As a newspaper account later stated: "It took rescue workers with equipment made for such gruesome tasks about fifteen minutes to get the dead man's leg out of the wreckage."

For their unselfish acts in freeing bus riders, and their desperate attempts to save the bus driver's life while facing danger to their own, Alaskans David Lancaster and Tom Burgess received the State of Alaska Award for Bravery-Heroism from Governor Walter Hickel in 1994. Medals were presented at the Capitol Building in Juneau.

Several other presentations honored the rescuers in the following months. All three men received the Emergency Medical Services Citizen Award, and Lancaster accepted the Soldier's Medal—the highest award for noncombat bravery.

The attempt to rescue Mike Rogers lives long in the memories of the men. Brantley returned to family in Georgia as manager of Mount Zion Automotive in Carrollton. Even to this day, when he thinks of the crash, a never-ending feeling of despair sweeps over him. He always wishes he had done more for Rogers.

Lancaster transferred to Fort McClellan in Alabama. Leaving Alaska helped him, and also moving closer to Brantley, who shared the experience. Though in different states, they live only fifty miles apart.

A couple of years after the disaster, an attorney called Lancaster back to Alaska to give a taped deposition about the accident. Legalities on behalf of Rogers's daughter were pending in the courts. Having to detail events in writing, Lancaster concluded, aided him in working through the nightmare of Rogers's death. "That helped," he said, "and talking it through with several military doctors."

Now retired from the Army, but still a trainer for the military, Lancaster said distance and time have helped to soothe his mind. But he never forgets, recalling the tragedy in subtle ways. "You'd be surprised at all the people in this world who have the name 'Mike Rogers,'" he said.

Even the simplest chores bring back the horror: "You go out and burn some papers or you see some fire and you're reminded." But the passing of years has helped. He remembered how beautifully that day began. "I try to think of the beginning, not the end."

To the present time, nightmares about the disaster plague Tom Burgess, who still lives in Fairbanks. "Sometimes," he said, "I 'what if' myself to death. It was such a helpless feeling knowing you couldn't do anything."

The rescuers saved several people on the Parks Highway that day, at very real risk to their own survival. Yet while others congratulated the men for their unselfish bravery, they did not think of themselves as heroes. Instead they blamed themselves for Mike Rogers's death. "We lost it and he was counting on us," Lancaster said.

As Robert Brantley so thoughtfully added, "There were no heroes out there. Only tragedy." ★

★

# NO TIME FOR FEAR

## Kenai, 1982

The workday over and night activities beginning, traffic proved fairly heavy along Kenai highways one October evening in 1982. Short days brought early darkness to the highways, and snow and cold added more dangers to poor visibility and slippery roads.

David Graham, family man and driller for an Amoco oil refinery, drove south on his way to the North Star United Methodist Church. He watched carefully as his 1966 yellow Mustang followed a string of cars along the Spur Highway, well aware of the dangerous road conditions. Because of this, Graham eased down on the brake well before approaching the intersection. The car ahead had its signal blinking for a left-hand turn onto Island Lake Road.

Behind Graham drove Sherry Collinsworth of Nikiski, returning home from a grocery-shopping trip. She, too, slowed as her Mercury station wagon neared the corner.

Behind Collinsworth, driving downhill at least forty-five miles per hour—way too fast for conditions—traveled John Reese in a 1974 Chevrolet. At that speed, there was no time to stop on the slippery road surface. The speeding car screeched along the ice and slammed into the rear of Collinsworth's Mercury. Her auto clipped the left rear fender of Graham's car, spinning him around, and then skidded across the intersection, hit a stopped car at the intersection, and landed into a ditch, a fire flaring up at the back of the Mercury.

After the crash, shaken but unhurt, Graham glanced into the rearview mirror, only to spot Collinsworth's car already on fire. Intending to help, Graham pulled to the side and parked. Another driver on the scene—Tylea A. Spurgin—also ran to the burning car to do what she could. She said something to Graham about the "driver still being in the car."

Graham dashed to the driver's door and saw Collinsworth inside, aware, but in shock, fighting to undo her seat belt. Graham tore at the door, but it would not open—the crash had jammed it shut. "I tried to get out the front doors," Collinsworth told the *Peninsula Clarion*, "but I kept fainting."

Graham ran around the car and tried the front passenger door, but it would not open either. He leaned over and jerked at the back passenger door. By now

Governor Bill Sheffield presents the medal to David Graham
while Suzette Graham looks on.

flames raged at the rear, licking underneath at the back wheels. The heat burned at his face and the roar drummed through his head. Graham knew he was running out of time; at any moment the whole car might explode. But he could not leave the driver in that furnace to burn to death without trying to help.

Again he yanked frantically at the back handle, kicking at the center door panel. Yanked again—kicked. Over and over. The pulling and constant pummeling buckled the panel in, the edges eased outward, and the door finally screeched opened. Would there be time? By now flames engulfed the total rear of the car.

Graham leaped inside the back, heavy smoke filling the interior, tearing his eyes, burning his throat, making it difficult to breathe. From what he could tell, Collinsworth passed in and out of consciousness. He shook her shoulder and shouted each word at her, "Get—out—of—the—car!"

The urgency forced Collinsworth alert. She leaned back, twisted around, and, with Graham pulling, struggled over the back seat and stumbled out of the car. She staggered to the side of the road in a daze and dropped in a snowbank. When Graham freed himself from the burning auto, he helped Collinsworth up, supported her to his car, and eased her inside. He knew shock gripped the woman, and he turned up the heater to full power.

Collinsworth taken care of, Graham stood back and watched the flaming car, being sure everyone else stood clear. He then checked the other accident victims to see if they were hurt and, moments later, helped direct traffic to avoid another collision.

By then, medics from Fire Station No. 2 had arrived; it was turning into a busy night for them. The medics placed Collinsworth in the ambulance and sped her to Central Peninsula General Hospital, where she remained for several hours until doctors released her. Collinsworth rested in bed the following week, as her jolting aches and pains healed. Incredibly, she was not burned at all. The car, however, totally melted inside, everything from dashboard to seats to steering wheel. She later reported that the driver who caused the crash had no insurance.

A trooper on the scene, Tom Preshaw, recommended Graham for commendation: "He risked serious harm to himself by entering the Collinsworth vehicle and pulling Collinsworth from the burning vehicle. In doing so, he saved Collinsworth's life."

Graham's wife, Suzette, was first to learn that the Alaska medal would be presented to her husband. She kept it a secret from him, until she took him to Anchorage for the award ceremonies. There, in February, Graham received the State of Alaska Award for Bravery-Heroism from Governor Bill Sheffield.

"I find your willingness to come to the aid of another Alaskan commendable, and you are more than worthy of the state of Alaska's highest award," the Governor praised.

Today Collinsworth and her family still live in Nikiski. "There is no doubt in my mind," Collinsworth said of the ordeal, "that I would have died in the vehicle had not Graham pulled me out."

David Graham and his family continue living in the Kenai area, where he works for a Tesoro oil refinery. A reserved man, Graham does not think of himself as a hero. "I was young," he said. "I reacted instinctively, just doing what had to be done. I just put my life on the line one time. Others do it all the time."

He said the real heroes are the firefighters, the police officers, the rescue workers—those who face emergencies and possible death every day. ★

With his wife, Florence, by his side, Gene Snell receives his medal from Governor Tony Knowles during ceremonies in Juneau, December 2000.

# MORE STORIES OF
# MEDAL WINNERS

Researching thirty different incidents that resulted in Bravery-Heroism Awards was no small challenge. In many cases, the trail left behind included newspaper accounts, magazine articles, and many after-the-fact interviews. But in some cases, information was scarce, with little available beyond official documentation.

Despite the more skeletal nature of the stories in this section, no compilation of the chronology of this award would be complete without some mention—as best it can be obtained—of each incident and the award recipients.

Even with lean information, the details tend to fascinate. This section contains twelve snapshots of additional dramatic rescues. They come from all over the state, from Shishmaref and Emmonak to Juneau and Anchorage, and even an award for the bravery of a young Alaskan attending the U.S. Junior Olympics in New Orleans, Louisiana.

In fact, several of these stories involve young people performing acts of great bravery, from a twelve-year-old girl who died saving her mother to a thirteen-year-old who jumped into the icy Emmonak River to save a six-year-old he knew could not swim. Another young man lost his life in his attempt to rescue a six-year-old lost while wading in the Kotlik Slough. The lack of detail hardly diminishes these significant deeds.

★

# DODGING BROKEN LIVE WIRES

### North Kenai, 1977

A small plane, piloted by Richard Lafferty, with passenger Jeff Lanman, crashed while landing near Collier Carbon and Chemical Plant in an industrial area of North Kenai on Friday, August 19, 1977, taking down dangerous power lines. On the ground, dodging broken live wires, Michael Hancock bolted forward through showers of electrical sparks and pulled both men to safety.

Governor Hammond's State of Alaska Award for Bravery-Heroism citation to Hancock read: The rescues were "accomplished at great personal risk to your own life and safety. The crash, which occurred under conditions of patchy ground fog, brought down high voltage power lines which increased the danger of fire at the accident site and, additionally, carried the threat of electrocution of would-be rescuers." The citation and medal were mailed to Hancock in March of 1980, as personal contact could not be arranged.

★

# OFFICER AMBUSHED

### Craig, 1966

Near midnight on a freezing winter night in Southeast Alaska, Craig police were summoned to the home of William Cogo, who had been stabbed by a young man named Stanley Carle.

Chief of Police Gorden Madden and a fellow officer, forty-four-year-old Kenneth Nauska, began a perilous search in the dark for Carle, aware they presented targets for the fugitive. While Nauska shone his flashlight around the Cogo yard, he was ambushed, shot, and killed. After a long hunt, police caught Carle, who confessed to running away, secreting the gun, and hiding for a day under the main Libby Cannery building. After a hearing and conviction, Judge Richard Lauber sentenced Carle to twenty years in jail for second-degree murder.

For heroic action in the line of duty, Governor Walter Hickel granted the State of Alaska Award for Bravery-Heroism posthumously to Kenneth Nauska, presenting the medal to his wife in a Ketchikan ceremony on May 23, 1967.

★

# SAVING "THREE SMALL LIVES"

## Ketchikan, 1967

While baby-sitting for the Fred Guthrie family in Ketchikan, fifty-three-year-old Rosie Edenshaw saved the lives of the three Guthrie children during an apartment fire.

Volunteer Fire Chief Earl Palmer described it best in the *Ketchikan Daily News:*

> "On hearing one of the children yelling there was smoke, Mrs. Edenshaw raced up the stairs where she found heavy smoke coming from the master bedroom. She picked up one of the children who was in the hallway and removed her to safety. She then returned to the children's bedroom on the second floor and crawled on her hands and knees trying to find the other two children, which she did. One was under his bed and the other had crawled under the blankets at the foot of the bed.

> "Mrs. Edenshaw, not finding the children in the bed, could easily have thought they had gotten out, but she stayed and kept looking until she found them and removed them to safety."

Governor Walter Hickel presented the State of Alaska Award for Bravery-Heroism medal to Edenshaw in Ketchikan on November 16, 1967, with the words, "Mrs. Edenshaw's bravery in the face of such danger was responsible for the direct saving of three small lives, a feat for which she deserves the gratitude and recognition of all her fellow citizens."

★

# GIRL SAVES MOTHER, DIES

### Sitka, 1984

When an early Saturday morning fire raged through the second floor of an apartment building in Sitka, twelve-year-old Esther Farquhar ran to her mother's bedroom with a chain fire ladder.

As the *Daily Sitka Sentinel* reported: "She quickly unfurled the ladder and reportedly ordered her mother, who initially argued with her child about who should leave first, to climb down. 'No, you go first and I'll follow you,' Esther said, according to her mother's statement." Firefighters figured Esther decided to try and rescue others who were still inside, rather than immediately follow her mother down the ladder. The young girl died in the flames.

Governor Bill Sheffield presented the State of Alaska Award for Bravery-Heroism medal posthumously to the Farquhar family in 1984.

This tragedy proved a sad echo of a disaster that had occurred five years earlier. At that time in 1979, Esther's older sister, Ruth Ann, died in an accidental apartment fire two blocks away. Both fires happened on a Saturday, and three people died in each.

★

# FIRST ON A FIRE SCENE

### Anchorage, 1997

When twenty-one-year-old Timothy Eldridge visited his friend, eighteen-year-old William Luce, in an Anchorage apartment house, they heard a cry of "Fire!" coming from outside. Investigating, Eldridge saw smoke, immediately ran upstairs, and tried to break into a locked third-floor apartment door. At the same time, Luce scaled the balconies and entered the smoky room through a sliding glass door.

Luce unlocked the apartment's front door, and Eldridge burst in. Through the smoke, Eldridge spotted a disoriented man on a sofa. He dashed forward and dragged the much heavier man to the outside corridor for fresh air, while Luce located a dry chemical extinguisher, hurried to the kitchen, and worked at snuffing out a grease fire threatening the apartment, the occupant, and the wooden building.

By this time the fire department had arrived. Firefighters took over and eventually transported the dazed resident to Elmendorf 5040th Hospital, where he recovered.

On December 28, 2000, Governor Tony Knowles presented the State of Alaska Award for Bravery-Heroism to the men's relatives at a ceremony in Anchorage, as Eldridge currently works outside the state, and Lucas attends school in Texas.

★

# BOAT HARBOR FIRE

Juneau, 1995

It was nearly noon on April 4, 1995, in Juneau, at the Harris Boat Harbor. As Rick Gottwald, a Fish and Wildlife Protection officer, worked aboard the ship *Enforcer* docked there, he spotted a fire on a small boat tied across the way and shouted for someone to call 911. With no time to run around the winding dock, Gottwald jumped into the water, swam to the boat, and boarded. The owner, intoxicated and unresponsive to Gottwald's calls, held a burning sleeping bag over his head. Gottwald grabbed the bag and threw it overboard. Well aware the gasoline engine might explode any minute, the officer nevertheless doused a fire on the individual, plus put out other spot fires burning in the cabin.

A letter from the Department of Public Safety stated: "Because Gottwald had to jump into the cold water and swim to the other dock, and the fact that the vessel was made of fiberglass, contained a gasoline system, and had an unresponsive, intoxicated person aboard, Gottwald's own safety was put in jeopardy." Governor Tony Knowles presented the State of Alaska Award for Bravery-Heroism in July of 1995, adding his own congratulations.

★

# "I HAD TO GET THE KID OUT . . ."

Emmonak, 1985

On an afternoon in September 1985, on his way home from school, thirteen-year-old Bill Westlock saw six-year-old Larry Wasuli fall into the icy Emmonak River outside the town of Emmonak in western Alaska. Bill knew Larry could not swim, and only one thought flashed through his mind: "I had to get the kid out of the water," which he did at risk to his own life.

As Governor Bill Sheffield's award letter stated: "Billy Westlock, completely forgetting his own safety, jumped right into the deep and freezing water after Larry and saved his life after a struggle to overcome the weight of the boy, his sodden clothes, and his hip boots that had filled with water." Sheffield presented the State of Alaska Award for Bravery-Heroism to Westlock at Emmonak City Hall the following year.

★

# THROUGH THE SEA ICE

Shishmaref, 1996

On a late November day in 1996, in freezing weather and blowing snow, snowmachiners John Sinnock and his son Ralph broke through the ocean ice near Shishmaref and plunged into the water. Ralph managed to swim to safe ice and hurried to Shishmaref for the Emergency Services. Twenty-two snowmachiners motored five miles out on the ice and, through poor visibility, began hunting in toward shore for the victim. Eventually searchers located Sinnock about one-quarter mile from Shishmaref, gripping his floating sled.

Gene Snell, one of the rescue crew, immediately jumped into the ocean, dog paddling to the victim. Snell yanked several times on Sinnock's hands to get him to release his grip from the sled. When he did, Snell struggled with

Sinnock to safe ice, where the rescue unit pulled them from the water. Both were hurried to the local clinic, and survived.

For his selfless act of courage, Gene Snell received the State of Alaska Award for Bravery-Heroism from Governor Tony Knowles in Anchorage, December 28, 2000. During the presentation, Snell said, "Best not to show fear or panic. But it was something that I did that was spontaneous. It's real hard to describe from deep inside. It's really hard to describe, period."

★

# "I KNEW THEY WERE IN TROUBLE . . ."

Juneau, 1997

Weather gave no thought to contestants fishing in the 51st Salmon Derby outside Juneau during a summer weekend in 1997. A small craft advisory warned of rain, six-foot seas, and twenty-five-knot winds blasting the area that Friday, August 5.

Heading for the North Douglas ramp in their nineteen-footer, Bob Janes and Jim Griffin plowed through heavy seas when suddenly their 110-horse-power Johnson lost power. Taking water over the transom, they tried to get a Mayday out, but the roiling waves soon capsized them, dumping them into the icy bay.

Captain Rick Siangco, on his thirty-two-footer some ten stormy minutes away, spotted the accident. "When I saw the bow go straight up into the air, I knew they were in trouble." Eventually, Siangco and his crew worked their way to the victims and pulled them out. "I knew they had already said their good-byes, but we were able to pull them out alive," Siangco added.

Governor Tony Knowles added his congratulations at presentation ceremonies in Anchorage on December 28, 2000, when he granted the State of Alaska Award for Bravery-Heroism to Rick Siangco.

★

# A FATAL ATTEMPT

### Kotlik, 1993

While wading in the shallows of Kotlik Slough in July 1993, six-year-old Jennifer Prince stepped out too far into deep water. Nearby, chopping wood for a steam-bath fire, Clyde Aketachunak, twenty-seven, and Alfred Andrews looked across and saw Jennifer in trouble. While Alfred went for help, Clyde dove in to save the little girl, in spite of having recently broken his collarbone.

A neighbor on the other side of the slough saw Clyde surface once with the girl, and then disappear.

Forty-five minutes later rescuers located the two bodies, and, at the time, Aketachunak clearly was dead. With hope the little girl might still be saved, village health aides flew her to the Bethel hospital, but a medical team could not bring her around.

Because of this unselfish act, giving his life attempting to save a little girl, Governor Walter Hickel awarded the State of Alaska Award for Bravery-Heroism posthumously to Aketachunak in 1994.

★

# "REMARKABLE" RESCUE

### North Pole, 1994

It was dusky outside, even an hour after midnight on a summer evening, when fourteen-year-old Travis Bennett and his mother, near their home, heard screams for help from the swift-flowing Chena River outside North Pole. A woman had fallen from a stranded boat into the swirling river. Promptly, Travis ran into his house, grabbed a rope, charged across the ice-cold slough, and found Debbie Peterson clutching a tree root in a swift part of the river. Travis gripped a hand—it slipped from his grasp. Quickly he grabbed the other just as she let go of the root, and passed the rope to her. Then Travis pulled her to shore, saving her life even though he, himself, might have been swept into the current.

North Pole volunteer Fire Chief Tim Biggane later said of Travis Bennett: "To be able to go out at that age and to be prepared to deal with the situation when he got there was remarkable." Governor Walter Hickel agreed, presenting the State of Alaska Award for Bravery-Heroism to Bennett on November 30, 1994.

★

# POOL RESCUE

### From Eagle River to New Orleans, 1996

Flying to New Orleans in August 1996 to compete in karate at the U.S. Junior Olympic Games proved a highlight for Sam Hoger, sixteen, and Joe Sinclair, ten, of Eagle River, Alaska. While both enjoyed free time with others in a private backyard swimming pool one afternoon, Sinclair, who could not swim, slipped off a rubber raft at the deep end. No one saw this, but Hoger spotted Sinclair at the bottom of the pool, dove in, and brought him to the surface.

While someone called 911, an older man applied CPR and revived Sinclair. An ambulance finally transported him to the emergency room, where he was treated for low oxygen blood levels and water in the lungs. After a night in the hospital and a doctor's OK, Sinclair was allowed to compete in the karate event the next day, winning a bronze medal.

Sam Hoger did not earn a medal in his event at the Junior Olympics, but his saving of Joe Sinclair translated into a much larger accomplishment. Hoger received his own trophy—the State of Alaska Award for Bravery-Heroism—from Governor Tony Knowles in October the same year.

Interestingly enough, Mrs. Sinclair reported that years before, Joe's uncle had died when he was only fourteen, while attempting to save someone from drowning. ★

# STATE OF ALASKA AWARD
# FOR BRAVERY-HEROISM

## Chronology*

1965—August 16, Albert Rothfuss, Ketchikan ("Special Delivery")
1966—January 29, Kenneth G. Nauska, Craig ("Officer Ambushed")
1967—October 6, Rosie Edenshaw, Ketchikan ("Saving 'Three Small Lives'")
1968—May 11, Randy Prinzing, Soldotna ("No Other Choice")
1971—October 18, Nancy Davis, over Alaska and the Northwest ("Skyjacked!")
1972—January 20, Jeffrey Stone, Fairbanks ("No Second Chance")
1975—August 30, Gilbert Pelowook and Gambell residents, Saint Lawrence Island, ("Beyond the Call")
1977—August 5, George Jackinsky, Kasilof ("Return from Death")
1977—August 19, Michael Hancock, Kenai ("Dodging Broken Live Wires")
1982—October 2, David Graham, Kenai ("No Time for Fear")
1983—January 14, John Stimson and Robert Larson, Cordova ("It's Now or Never")
1984—April 7, Esther Farquhar, Sitka ("Girl Saves Mother, Dies")
1984—September 22, Darin Olanna, Nome ("'He Gave His Life to Save a Friend . . .'")
1985—September 4, Bill Westlock, Emmonak ("'I Had to Get the Kid Out . . .'")
1987—December 10, John Whiddon, Carl Saylor, Greg Breithaupt, Jeff Tunks, Mark Milne, near Sitka ("The Very Edge of Death")
1988—June 2, Alaska Army National Guard members, off Saint Lawrence Island, ("Adrift to Nowhere")
1989—October 15, Evans Geary, Jessie Ahkpuk Jr., Johnny Sheldon, Jason Rutman, Buckland ("Fight for Life")
1990—July 1, Robert Cusack, Lake Iliamna ("Against All Odds")
1991—May 8, Keith Comer, Bob Yerex, Gary Strebe, Dave Schron, Jeff Waite, off Kodiak ("Last Voyage of the *Dora H.*")
1993—July 14, David Lancaster, Tom Burgess, near Talkeetna ("From Beautiful Day . . . to Nightmare")
1993—July 14, Clyde Aketachunak, Kotlik ("A Fatal Attempt")
1993—August 13, Eric Pentilla, Walter Greaves, Randy Oles, Jerry Austin, Nome ("Doing It the Hard Way")
1994—June 22, Mike Olsen, Russell Shaub, Kevin Kramer, George Coulter, Juneau ("No Turning Back")
1994—June 30, Travis Bennett, North Pole ("'Remarkable' Rescue")
1995—February 17, Rose Edgren, Delta Junction ("The Quick or the Dead")
1995—April 4, Rick Gottwald, Juneau ("Boat Harbor Fire")
1996—August 8, Sam Hoger, from Eagle River to New Orleans ("Pool Rescue")
1996—November 8, Gene Snell, Shishmaref ("Through the Sea Ice")
1997—June 29, Timothy Eldridge, William Luce, Anchorage ("First on a Fire Scene")
1997—August 5, Rick Siangco, Juneau ("'I Knew They Were in Trouble . . .'")

* *Dates are when rescues occurred, not when the heroism medals were presented.*

# ABOUT THE AUTHOR

Researching the stories in this book took persistence, says writer Nancy Warren Ferrell. While the idea for the collection came from an acquaintance, once she began the project, Ferrell dug in like a detective. She relied on government entities such as fire departments, aviation agencies, the U.S. Coast Guard, local police, and state troopers to provide information and photographs. Once she had the details, she used the Internet to find phone numbers to track down heroes for interviews.

While she always read and used news accounts, letters, and any official reports available on these events, Ferrell says there was no substitute for speaking firsthand with a hero or the survivor. These personal accounts always brought out more human details not covered in reports. "The sheer courage made me shake my head in wonder," she says.

A resident of Juneau, Alaska, for thirty-five years, Ferrell has written nine nonfiction books for young people, three for adults.

# SOURCES

## Magazines, Journals, Flyers

*Air Line Pilot*

*Alaska* magazine

Strickland, Don. "George Jackinsky—
The Man Behind the Medal." March
1980, p. A19.

Whiddon, John, "The Seaworthy and
the Brave." Dec. 1989, p. 58.

Davidson, Art, "Adrift in Bering Sea."
Oct. 1989, p. 37.

*Alaska Fisherman's Journal*

*Alaska Bear*

Haley, Christopher E., "Bluebird
Sinks." Jan-Mar. 1988, p. 8.

Jones, Dean, "Air Station Kodiak vs.
Mother Nature." Apr.-May 1991, p. 14.

*DMVA Impact* (Dept. Of Military and
Veterans Affairs)

Haller, Lt. Mike, "Walrus Hunters
Survive." Jan. 1989.

Gard, Wanda. Unpublished narrative.
(Undated)

*General Aviation News & Flyer Intercom*
(FAA newsletter)

Jacobsen, Bob. Symposium presentation.
(Undated)

*Reader's Digest*

SS *Arizona Standard* (ship newsletter)

Taku Lodge Flyer

The Marshall Community *Ad-Visor*

*Wilderness and Environmental Medicine*

Russell, Alex B. "Aircraft Down." 2,
1996, p. 190.

## Books:

*Alaska Atlas & Gazetteer.* Freeport, Me.:
DeLorme Mapping, 1992.

*Alaska's Seward Peninsula.* Alaska
Geographic Society, 1987.

Anderson and Rohrer. *The Rescue.*
Tempe, Ariz.: Fellowship Publishing,
1995.

Orth, Donald. *Dictionary of Alaska Place
Names.* Washington D.C.: Goverment
Printing Office, 1967.

Pearson, Roger. *Alaska in Maps.*
Fairbanks: Univeristy of Alaska, 1998.

Salisbury, C.A. *Soldiers of the Mists.*
Missoula, Mont.: Pictorial Histories
Co., 1992.

*World Almanac and Book of Facts, 1995.*
Mahwah, N.J.: World Almanac, 1994.

*World Atlas.* Hammond Publications,
1984.

## Television

KINY-TV, Morning news from
Anchorage, December 29, 2000.

Video: "The Rescue," A Light Sounds
Production, Anchorage. Fellowship
Ministries, 1999.

## Newspapers

*Anchorage Daily News*
*Anchorage Times*
*Anniston Star*
*Arctic Sounder*
*Boston Globe*
*Chugiak-Eagle River Star*
*Cordova Times*
*Daily News* (Newport, Massachusetts)
*Daily Sitka Sentinel*
*Delta Wind*
*Fairbanks Daily News-Miner*
*Frontiersman*
*Juneau Empire*
*Kenai Peninsula Cheechako News*
*Ketchikan Daily News*
*Kodiak Mirror*
*Kodiak Daily Mirror*
*McClellan News*
*New Orleans Times-Picayune*
*Nome Nugget*
*Northwest Arctic NUNA*
*Peninsula Clarion*
*Southeast Alaska Empire*
*Sequim Gazette*
*Tacoma News Tribune*
*Tundra Drums*
*Tundra Times*
*Yukon Sentinel*

# INDEX

Italic page numbers indicate photographs